The International Highrise Award 2020
Internationaler Hochhaus Preis 2020

Edited by Herausgegeben von
Peter Körner, Stefanie Lampe,
Jonas Malzahn, Peter Cachola Schmal

      jovis

Contents Inhalt

Foreword

Foreword

Dr. Ina Hartwig
Deputy Mayor in Charge of Culture of the City of
Frankfurt am Main

Dr. Matthias Danne
Deputy CEO of DekaBank

Peter Cachola Schmal
Director, Deutsches Architekturmuseum (DAM)

This year, 31 projects from 14 countries were nominated for the International Highrise Award. As in previous years, nowhere else in the world have so many high-rise buildings been built as in China. About one in three towers with a height of at least 100 meters is still being built in China, with more and more local architects being involved. This enormous construction activity is also reflected in the list of nominees, which includes ten projects in China. In many countries, especially in China, delays occurred as a result of the COVID-19 pandemic: projects were not submitted because buildings could not be occupied or current pictures could no longer be taken. Although preliminary research by Deutsches Architekturmuseum showed a slight decline in completions worldwide, partly due to the 2008 financial crisis, the typology of high-rise buildings is increasingly becoming established in all parts of the world. European cities are now pushing ahead with high-rise development, and new towers are also being built successively in Africa, as evidenced by the first nomination of a project on this continent, or more precisely in Morocco.

While the first three winners of the International Highrise Award were still purely office towers (in 2004 De Hoftoren in The Hague by Kohn Pedersen Fox, in 2006 Torre Agbar in Barcelona by Ateliers Jean Nouvel, in 2008 Hearst Headquarters in New York by Foster + Partners), the winners of the last few years clearly reflect the trend towards the high-rise residential building. Even though it was again office towers, 1 Bligh Street in Sydney by ingenhoven architects + Architectus in 2012 and Torre Reforma by L. Benjamín Romano in 2018, which impressed the jury with their outstanding

Vorwort

Dr. Ina Hartwig
Kulturdezernentin der Stadt Frankfurt am Main

Dr. Matthias Danne
Stellvertretender Vorsitzender des Vorstands der
DekaBank

Peter Cachola Schmal
Direktor des Deutschen Architekturmuseums

In diesem Jahr wurden 31 Projekte aus 14 Ländern für die Auszeichnung mit dem Internationalen Hochhaus Preis nominiert. Wie auch in den Jahren zuvor entstanden nirgends auf der Welt so viele Hochhäuser wie in China. Nach wie vor wird ungefähr jedes dritte Gebäude mit einer Höhe von mindestens 100 Metern im Reich der Mitte gebaut, wobei vermehrt lokale Architekten zum Zuge kommen. Diese enorme Bautätigkeit spiegelt sich auch in der Liste der Nominierten wider, die zehn Projekte in China beinhaltet. In vielen Ländern, besonders in China, kam es aufgrund der COVID-19-Pandemie zu einigen Verzögerungen: Projekte wurden nicht eingereicht, weil Gebäude nicht bezogen oder keine aktuellen Bilder mehr erstellt werden konnten. Obwohl die Vorrecherche des Deutschen Architekturmuseums weltweit einen leichten Fertigstellungsrückgang verzeichnete, der unter anderem auf die Finanzkrise von 2008 zurückzuführen ist, etabliert sich die Typologie Hochhaus vermehrt in allen Teilen der Welt. So treiben mittlerweile europäische Städte ihre Hochhausentwicklung voran, und auch in Afrika entstehen sukzessive neue Türme, was die erstmalige Nominierung eines Projekts auf diesem Kontinent, in Marokko, belegt.

Nachdem die ersten drei Preisträger des Internationalen Hochhaus Preises noch reine Bürotürme waren (2004 De Hoftoren in Den Haag von Kohn Pedersen Fox, 2006 Torre Agbar in Barcelona von Ateliers Jean Nouvel, 2008 Hearst Headquarters in New York von Foster + Partners), bilden die Gewinner der letzten Jahre die Entwicklung zum Wohnhochhaus deutlich ab. Auch wenn 2012 mit 1 Bligh Street in Sydney von ingenhoven architects + Architectus sowie 2018 mit dem Torre Reforma von L. Benjamín Romano noch einmal zwei Bürotürme durch ihre herausragende architektonische

International Highrise Award 2020: Jury session at DAM, Frankfurt am Main
Jurysitzung des Internationalen Hochhaus Preises 2020 im DAM, Frankfurt am Main

architectural quality, the focus since 2010 has increasingly been on residential use. As a result, the high-rises awarded in 2010, The Met in Bangkok by WOHA, in 2014, Bosco Verticale in Milan by Stefano Boeri, and in 2016, VIA 57 West in New York by BIG—Bjarke Ingels Group, were purely residential projects.

Following the major metropolises in North America and Asia, this trend is now also reaching Europe. This year's prize winner, Norra Tornen by the Office for Metropolitan Architecture (OMA) in Rotterdam, is located in Sweden's capital Stockholm. There the award-winning project creates a gate situation to the Hagastaden district. With their excellent execution and the predominant use of prefabricated concrete elements, the city's tallest residential buildings cultivate living at height with a pronounced reference to the exterior in northern Europe.

In accordance with the statutes, this year's prize winner was again chosen from five finalists. Although three of the five projects are mainly dedicated to housing, it is striking that no specific 'type' of high-rise residential buildings can be discerned—all projects are distinguished by an individual signature that responds to highly diverse local requirements.

Omniturm in Frankfurt by BIG—Bjarke Ingels Group from New York / Copenhagen is the first mixed-use high-rise building in Germany to qualify as a finalist. The building's characteristic hip swing is a sign of the incipient change in downtown Frankfurt, which is dominated by office towers.

Once again, a project in Singapore is among the finalists. Shell-shaped planters make EDEN by Heatherwick Studio from London a memorable example of a residential tower. Its lavish planting impressively demonstrates the qualities that the urban development motto of *City in a Garden* puts into words.

Skidmore, Owings & Merrill from New York, otherwise known worldwide for their height records, is among the finalists with another residential project. The Stratford in London combines a design

Qualität überzeugten, liegt der Fokus seit 2010 vermehrt auf dem Wohnen. So wurden 2010 mit The Met in Bangkok von WOHA, 2014 mit dem Bosco Verticale in Mailand von Stefano Boeri sowie 2016 mit VIA 57 West in New York von BIG – Bjarke Ingels Group reine Wohnprojekte ausgezeichnet.

Nach den großen Metropolen in Nordamerika und Asien kommt dieser Trend nun auch in Europa an. Der diesjährige Preisträger Norra Tornen von Office for Metropolitan Architecture (OMA) aus Rotterdam steht in Schwedens Hauptstadt Stockholm. Dort bildet das prämierte Projekt eine Torsituation zum Stadtteil Hagastaden. Dabei kultivieren die höchsten Wohngebäude der Stadt durch ihre exzellente Ausführung sowie den überwiegenden Einsatz von Betonfertigteilen das Wohnen in der Höhe mit ausgeprägtem Außenbezug im Norden Europas.

Auch in diesem Jahr ging der Preisträger gemäß den Statuten aus fünf Finalisten hervor. Obwohl drei der fünf Projekte mehrheitlich dem Wohnen gewidmet sind, fällt auf, dass kein spezifischer „Typ" von Wohnhochhäusern zu erkennen ist – alle Projekte zeichnen sich durch eine individuelle Handschrift aus, die auf unterschiedlichste Anforderungen vor Ort reagiert.

Mit dem Frankfurter Omniturm von BIG – Bjarke Ingels Group aus New York / Kopenhagen hat es das erste gemischt genutzte Hochhaus Deutschlands unter die Finalisten geschafft. Der charakteristische Hüftschwung des Gebäudes ist ein Zeichen für den beginnenden Wandel in der von Bürotürmen dominierten Frankfurter Innenstadt.

Erneut zählt ein Projekt aus Singapur zu den Finalisten. Muschelförmige Pflanzkübel machen EDEN von Heatherwick Studio aus London zum einprägsamen Beispiel für ein Wohnhochhaus. Und mit seiner verschwenderischen Bepflanzung zeigt es eindrucksvoll die Qualitäten, die das Motto der Stadtentwicklung „City in a Garden" in Worte fasst.

Mit einem weiteren Wohnprojekt ist das sonst für seine Höhenrekorde weltweit bekannte Büro Skidmore, Owings & Merrill aus New York unter den Finalisten vertreten. The Stratford in London vereint Design-Hotel und Design-Wohnen unter einem Dach und setzt neue

hotel and design apartments under one roof and adds new urban development accents in the district of the same name. The distinctive large-scale form with deep recesses makes the building a landmark visible from afar in the area around the Queen Elizabeth Olympic Park in the east of the city, which was created for the 2012 Summer Olympics.

An outstanding structural achievement is Leeza SOHO in Beijing by Zaha Hadid Architects, whose glass envelope actually conceals a twin-tower layout. The more than 190-meter high atrium between the towers is the tallest in the world, and its fascinating curved shapes could only be achieved by means of parametric design.

The International Highrise Award was jointly initiated in 2003 by the City of Frankfurt, Deutsches Architekturmuseum, and DekaBank, and was presented for the first time in 2004. It has since been cooperatively organized and financed on a biennial basis and is awarded for the ninth time this year. Due to the COVID-19 pandemic, preparations for the award took place under very different circumstances. The worldwide travel restrictions required a local jury for the first time, before it became clear that it would not be possible to implement this either and the jury meeting had to be held digitally. The festive award ceremony in Frankfurt's Paulskirche in front of a large audience has to be reconsidered—we have taken the Corona crisis as an opportunity to dare something new and plan a hybrid event that will use digital channels to reach a much larger, more international audience.

High-rise construction has a long tradition in Frankfurt. The skyline, which has been expanding since the Second World War, was for decades not only unique in Germany but also trend-setting for Europe. Due to the limited building land available and the growing demand for office space, an inner-city density became necessary that could only be achieved with this building type. Today, highrises characterize the cityscape and symbolize the success and self-confidence of our small metropolis. This year, two projects located in Frankfurt are among the nominees, which bear witness to both the continuing boom in high-rise construction and the trend towards residential use.

With its ongoing commitment to the International Highrise Award, the **City of Frankfurt** underscores its consistent stance according to which not just every meter of height is crucial in high-rise construction but also convincing overall concepts in terms of economy, integration into the urban context, design, technology, and quality of stay. Special attention is increasingly being paid to ecological aspects. The International Highrise Award is thus aimed at buildings with a minimum height of 100 meters, which represent outstanding contributions to the evolution of the category of high-rise architecture worldwide.

For DekaBank, the presentation of the International Highrise Award has been an important part of its social commitment since the joint establishment 17 years ago. The award has gained international

städtebauliche Akzente im Stadtteil gleichen Namens. Die markante Großform mit tiefen Einschnitten macht das Gebäude zum weithin sichtbaren Wahrzeichen in der Gegend rund um den für Olympia 2012 entstandenen Queen Elizabeth Olympic Park im Osten der Stadt.

Eine herausragende Tragwerksleistung ist das Leeza SOHO von Zaha Hadid Architects in Peking, dessen Glashülle eigentlich eine Doppelturmanlage verbirgt. Das über 190 Meter hohe Atrium zwischen den Türmen ist das höchste der Welt, und seine faszinierenden geschwungenen Formen sind nur mithilfe des parametrischen Entwerfens möglich.

Der Internationale Hochhaus Preis wurde 2003 gemeinsam von der Stadt Frankfurt am Main, dem Deutschen Architekturmuseum und der DekaBank initiiert und 2004 zum ersten Mal ausgelobt. Seitdem wird er alle zwei Jahre kooperativ organisiert und finanziert und in diesem Jahr somit zum neunten Mal vergeben. Die Vorbereitungen für den Preis fanden aufgrund der weltweiten Covid-19-Pandemie unter stark geänderten Vorzeichen statt. Die weltweiten Reisebeschränkungen erforderten erstmalig eine lokale Jury, bevor dann klar war, dass sich auch dies nicht würde umsetzen lassen, und die Jurysitzung digital stattfand. Die feierliche Preisverleihung in der Frankfurter Paulskirche vor großem Publikum muss neu gedacht werden – wir nahmen die Corona-Krise zum Anlass, Neues zu wagen und eine hybride Veranstaltung zu planen, die über digitale Kanäle ein weit größeres, internationaleres Publikum erreichen soll.

In Frankfurt am Main hat der Hochhausbau Tradition. Die seit dem Zweiten Weltkrieg wachsende Skyline war über Jahrzehnte nicht nur singulär in Deutschland, sondern auch richtungsweisend für Europa. Aufgrund der begrenzten Bauflächen und der wachsenden Nachfrage nach Büroräumen wurde eine innerstädtische Dichte erforderlich, die nur mit diesem Gebäudetyp erreicht werden konnte. Heute prägen die Hochhäuser das Stadtbild und symbolisieren den Erfolg und das Selbstbewusstsein unserer kleinen Metropole. Dieses Jahr befinden sich gleich zwei Frankfurter Projekte unter den Nominierten, die von dem anhaltenden Hochhausboom sowie der Hinwendung zum Wohnen zeugen.

Mit dem andauernden Engagement für den Internationalen Hochhaus Preis verdeutlicht die Stadt Frankfurt am Main ihre konsequente Haltung, wonach im Hochhausbau nicht allein die Höhenmeter, sondern überzeugende Gesamtkonzepte in Bezug auf Wirtschaftlichkeit, Einbindung in den urbanen Kontext, Design und Technik sowie Aufenthaltsqualität maßgebend sind. Ein besonderes Augenmerk liegt in zunehmendem Maße auf ökologischen Aspekten. Somit richtet sich der Internationale Hochhaus Preis an Bauten mit einer Mindesthöhe von 100 Metern, die herausragende Beiträge zur Evolution der Gattung Hochhausarchitektur weltweit darstellen.

Für die DekaBank ist die Verleihung des Internationalen Hochhaus Preises seit der gemeinsamen Gründung vor 17 Jahren ein wichtiger Teil ihres gesellschaftlichen Engagements. Durch die kontinuierliche Weiterentwicklung des Preises und die dabei gewachsene, vertrauens-

Thomas Demand,
prize winner's
sculpture for the
International Highrise
Award Statuette für
den Internationalen
Hochhaus Preis,
titanium and granite
Titan und Granit,
36 x 15 x 12 cm

recognition through its continuous development and the matured, trusting cooperation between the three partners. DekaBank, the investment division of the Sparkasse financial group, together with its subsidiaries forms the Deka Group and is among the largest asset managers in Germany. With its involvement in the International Highrise Award, Deka aims to shift the focus to innovative, forward-looking, sustainable and economical construction.

Since the beginning of the millennium, Deutsches Architekturmuseum (DAM) has been accompanying the worldwide boom in the architectural showcase discipline of the 21st century. In the context of the biennial awarding of the award, a long-term analysis of the contemporary development of high-rise buildings including an informative documentation is emerging.

It will be exciting to see how the necessary social distancing rules will influence not only social interaction in the near future but also urban planning, landscape architecture, the microclimate debate, and (high-rise) architecture as such. Will the continuous influx into the cities, which are growing ever denser, persist worldwide or will a reversal of this trend become apparent in the coming years? How will projects specifically designed for density, such as residential but also office towers, change in the next few years? How will the office high-rise develop in times of increased work in the home office?

volle Zusammenarbeit der drei Partner hat sich die Auszeichnung internationale Anerkennung erworben. Die DekaBank, das Wertpapierhaus der Sparkassen, bildet gemeinsam mit ihren Tochtergesellschaften die Deka-Gruppe und ist einer der größten Asset Manager in Deutschland. Mit ihrem Engagement für den Internationalen Hochhaus Preis möchte die Deka den Fokus auf innovatives, zukunftsweisendes, nachhaltiges und wirtschaftliches Bauen richten.

Das Deutsche Architekturmuseum (DAM) begleitet bereits seit Anfang des Jahrtausends den weltweit andauernden Boom der architektonischen Parade-disziplin des 21. Jahrhunderts. Im Kontext der zwei-jährlichen Vergabe des Preises entsteht eine Langzeitanalyse der zeitgenössischen Hochhaus-entwicklung mitsamt einer aussagekräftigen Dokumen-tation.

Es wird spannend sein, zu verfolgen, wie die gebotenen Abstandsregeln in naher Zukunft nicht nur die soziale Interaktion beeinflussen werden, sondern auch den Städtebau, die Landschaftsarchitektur, die Mikroklima-Debatte und die (Hochhaus-)Architektur an sich. Wird sich der kontinuierliche Zuzug in die immer dichter werdenden Städte weltweit fortsetzen oder wird sich in den nächsten Jahren eine Trendumkehr abzeichnen? Wie werden sich gezielt auf Dichte ausgelegte Projekte, wie Wohn-, aber auch Bürohochhäuser, in den nächsten Jahren verändern? Wie wird sich das Bürohochhaus in Zeiten des verstärkten Arbeitens im Homeoffice entwickeln?

Jurors of the International Highrise Award 2020 Juroren des Internationalen Hochhaus Preises 2020 **From left to right** Von links nach rechts: **Anett-Maud Joppien (Architect** Architekt, **Co-Founder and managing director** Gründerin und Geschäftsführerin **Dietz Joppien Planungsgesellschaft, Frankfurt am Main); Klaus Fäth (Structural engineer** Bauingenieur, **Founder & Consultant** Gründer & Berater **office for structural design, Frankfurt am Main); Ina Hartwig (Deputy Mayor in charge of Culture** Kulturdezernentin, **Frankfurt am Main); Andreas Moser (Architect** Architekt, **Founder** Gründer **Cyrus Moser Architekten, Frankfurt am Main); Horst R. Muth (Head of Project & Development Management** Leiter Projekt-management Immobilien, **Deka Immobilien GmbH, Frankfurt am Main); L. Benjamín Romano (Architect** Architekt, **Founder** Gründer **LBR&A Arquitectos, Mexico City** Mexiko-Stadt**); Peter Cachola Schmal (Director** Direktor **Deutsches Architektur-museum DAM, Frankfurt am Main); Victor Stoltenburg (Managing Director/Head of Acquisitions and Sales** Geschäfts-führer/Leiter An- und Verkauf, **Deka Immobilien GmbH, Frankfurt am Main); Rudi Scheuermann (consultant without voting rights** Berater ohne Stimmrecht **Director and Global Leader Building Envelope Design, Arup, Berlin)**

While in previous years countless project boards adorned the executive floor of DekaBank in the Trianon high-rise, only a few tables with laptops positioned sufficiently far apart stood in the unusually empty auditorium of Deutsches Architekturmuseum for the jury meeting to decide on the winner of the International Highrise Award 2020 in April. Due to the COVID-19 pandemic and the associated travel and contact restrictions, this year, screens were set up to show the expectant faces of the jury members. Few had ever experienced a digital jury session before, so everyone was eagerly awaiting the new experience and how the format would prove itself. The jury had intensively studied the documents in the days before and was well-prepared.

The winner of the IHA 2018, Benjamin Romano, took part in the jury meeting in distant Mexico at 3:00 a.m. local time due to the time difference of seven hours. However, despite the night-time effort and the virtual meeting, the discussion was animated and controversial during the session chaired by Anett-Maud Joppien.

The issue of the ecological and social properties of the buildings proved to be of central importance. Many of the competition entries were also examined with regard to the building's resilience in terms of its structure and life cycle.

Due to the individual appearance of the finalists—whether "baroque and eccentric", as Frankfurt's Deputy Mayor in Charge of Culture, Ina Hartwig, described the entry from Heatherwick Studio in Singapore, or "unique due to a simple hip swing", as Deka real estate expert Horst R. Muth commented on the OMNITURM by BIG in Frankfurt—it was not easy to decide on the award winner.

In addition to the impressive atrium of the Leeza SOHO Tower by Zaha Hadid Architects, it was the flexibility and variety of possible uses that the jury deemed remarkable. According to consultant Rudi Scheuermann, one of the main reasons for this aspect of use is the 'superstructure' of the high-rise, which also ensures a high level of stability.

Ina Hartwig brought the demand for affordable living space also in high-rise construction into the focus of the jury meeting. It is therefore not surprising that the majority of finalists are high-rise buildings with residential use, albeit in a broad spectrum ranging from urban residential high-rise to luxury tower.

From this point of view, the apparently luxurious EDEN in Singapore and the more restrained Norra Tornen in Stockholm prove to be antipodes. Both projects were acclaimed by the jury for their individual approaches.

Norra Tornen finally came out on top because, as the jury emphasized, it is an expression of an equal society, which is not only a characteristic of Swedish culture but also a universal message.

Schmückten in den vergangenen Jahren unzählige Projekttafeln die Vorstandsetage der DekaBank im Trianon-Hochhaus, so standen für die Jurysitzung zur Vergabe des Internationalen Hochhaus Preises 2020 im April nur wenige, ausreichend weit voneinander entfernte Tische mit Laptops im ungewohnt leeren Auditorium des Deutschen Architekturmuseums. Aufgrund der COVID-19-Pandemie und damit einhergehenden Reise- und Kontaktbeschränkungen blickte man in diesem Jahr auf Bildschirmen in die erwartungsvollen Gesichter der Jurymitglieder. Nur wenige hatten jemals zuvor eine digitale Jurysitzung miterlebt, somit waren alle gespannt auf das neue Erlebnis und darauf, wie sich das Format bewähren würde. Die Jury hatte die Unterlagen in den Tagen zuvor intensiv studiert und war bestens vorbereitet.

Der Sieger des IHP 2018, Benjamin Romano, beteiligte sich im entfernten Mexiko aufgrund der Zeitverschiebung von sieben Stunden um drei Uhr morgens Ortszeit an der Jurysitzung. Doch trotz des nächtlichen Einsatzes und der nur virtuellen Begegnung wurde unter dem Vorsitz von Anett-Maud Joppien angeregt und kontrovers diskutiert.

Dabei erwies sich die Frage nach den ökologischen und sozialen Qualitäten der Gebäude als zentral. Auch der Aspekt der Resilienz in Bezug auf die Struktur und den Lebenszyklus eines Bauwerks wurde an vielen Wettbewerbsbeiträgen geprüft.

Aufgrund der individuellen Gestalt der Finalisten – ob „barock und exzentrisch", wie die Frankfurter Kulturdezernentin Ina Hartwig den Beitrag von Heatherwick Studio in Singapur beschrieb, oder „einzigartig durch einen einfachen Hüftschwung", so der Deka Immobilienexperte Horst R. Muth über den OMNITURM von BIG in Frankfurt – fiel die Entscheidung für den Preisträger nicht leicht.

Neben dem beeindruckenden Atrium des Leeza SOHO Tower von Zaha Hadid Architects war es die Flexibilität und Vielfalt der möglichen Nutzung, die die Jury für bemerkenswert hielt. Verantwortlich für diesen Nutzungsaspekt sei laut Berater Rudi Scheuermann nicht zuletzt die „Superstructure" des Hochhauses, die ihm auch ein hohes Maß an Resilienz verleihe.

Die Nachfrage nach bezahlbarem Wohnraum auch im Hochhausbau wurde von Ina Hartwig in den Fokus der Jurysitzung gerückt. Somit ist es nicht verwunderlich, dass die Mehrheit der Finalisten Hochhäuser mit Wohnnutzung sind; allerdings in einem breiten Spektrum von städtischem Wohnturm bis hin zum Luxus-Tower.

Unter diesem Gesichtspunkt erweisen sich das augenscheinlich als Luxusdomizil errichtete EDEN in Singapur und die zurückhaltenderen Norra Tornen in Stockholm als Antipoden. Beide Projekte wurden von der Jury für ihre individuellen Ansätze gelobt.

Die Norra Tornen setzen sich schließlich als Gewinner durch, da sie, wie die Jury hervorhob, Ausdruck einer gleichwertigen Gesellschaft seien, womit sie nicht nur ein Charakteristikum der schwedischen Kultur, sondern auch eine universelle Botschaft zum Ausdruck bringen.

The towers seem to be made of stacked boxes.
Die Türme scheinen wie aus Boxen gestapelt.

DAM Director Peter Cachola Schmal pointed out that Norra Tornen create a newly emerging gate situation that is shaping urban development. Nonetheless, the towers impress with their sculptural effect. Andreas Moser praised the elegance the high-rises have in emerging from the lower buildings surrounding them, and gave a positive assessment of the tension between the towers' brutalist appearance and their context. Rudi Scheuermann attested Norra Tornen a timeless design. The excellent materiality and design of the precast concrete elements, their ingenious joining, which creates exciting individual loggias, as well as the contrast to the fine details of the interior – Anett-Maud Joppien and Benjamin Romano agreed on this – are an absolutely unique characteristic.

DAM Direktor Peter Cachola Schmal wies darauf hin, dass Norra Tornen eine neu entstehende und städtebaulich prägende Torsituation ist, die durch ihre skulpturale Wirkung besteche. Andreas Moser lobte die Eleganz, mit der die Türme aus der sie umgebenden niedrigeren Bebauung hervorwachsen, und bewertete das Spannungsfeld zwischen der brutalistischen Erscheinung der Türme und ihrem Kontext positiv. Rudi Scheuermann attestierte Norra Tornen eine zeitlose Gestalt. Die exzellente Materialität und Ausführung der Betonfertigteilelemente, ihre geschickte Fügung, die spannende individuelle Loggien erzeugt, sowie der Kontrast zu den feinen Details der Innenräume seien – darin stimmten Benjamin Romano und Anett-Maud Joppien überein – ein absolutes Alleinstellungsmerkmal.

The glass parapets are
almost invisible.
Die gläsernen Brüstungen
sind nahezu unsichtbar.

View over Vasastaden with Norra Tornen – Innovationen in the foreground, while the second tower Helix was still under construction.
Blick über Vasastaden mit Norra Tornen – Innovationen im Vordergrund, während der zweite Turm Helix noch im Bau war.

Prize Winner 2020
Preisträger 2020

OMA Office for Metropolitan Architecture
NORRA TORNEN
Stockholm, Sweden Schweden

Architects Architekten OMA Office for Metropolitan
Architecture, Rotterdam/Beijing Peking, Netherlands
Niederlande/China
Project architects Projektarchitekten Reinier de Graaf,
Alex de Jong, Philippe Braun, Diana Cristobal, Roza
Matveeva, Edward Nicholson, Peter Rieff, Carolien
Schippers
Architects of record Lokale Architekten Tengbom
Client Bauherr Oscar Properties
Structural engineers Tragwerksplanung Arup
MEP Haustechnik Arup

Height Höhe Innovationen 125 m, Helix 110 m
Stories Geschosse 36, 32
Site area Grundstücksfläche 1235 m²
Building footprint Bebaute Fläche 1235 m²
Gross floor area Bruttogeschossfläche 31 826 m²
Structure Konstruktion Reinforced concrete with
prefabricated concrete modules Stahlbeton mit
vorgefertigten Betonmodulen
Completion Fertigstellung December Dezember 2018/
August 2020
Main use Hauptnutzung Residential Wohnen

Sustainability:
energy-efficient sandwich façade with 23-centimeter
insulation; triple-glazed windows using a single
sheet of glass without transoms and mullions
avoiding thermal bridges; natural ventilation; heat
recovery scheme; heat exchangers are installed in
each apartment or commercial unit; the buildings are
connected to the district cooling system; gray water
reuse; public transport nearby

Nachhaltigkeit:
energieeffiziente Sandwichfassade mit 23 cm dicker
Wärmedämmung; dreifachverglaste Fenster ohne Riegel
und Pfosten zur Vermeidung von Kältebrücken; natürliche Belüftung; Wärmerückgewinnungssystem; Wärmetauscher in jeder Wohnung oder Gewerbeeinheit;
Anschluss an das Fernkühlsystem; Grauwassernutzung;
gute Anbindung an den öffentlichen Nahverkehr

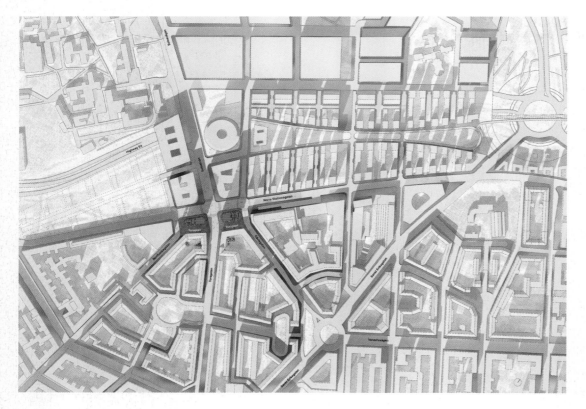

Site plan
Lageplan

On the Torsgatan arterial
road, the project marks
the transition between
the Vasastaden and
Hagastaden districts.
Auf der Ausfallstraße
Torsgatan markiert das
Projekt den Übergang
zwischen den Stadtteilen
Vasastaden und
Hagastaden.

The Norra Tornen twin towers, the 'northern towers', are located at the transition from Vasastaden, a district with residential developments mainly from the 1930s, to the newly emerging district of Hagastaden and create a gate situation to the left and right of the arterial road Torsgatan. A gate formed by two high-rise buildings is a motive traditionally used in Stockholm's cityscape to mark important points, for example the transition from one island to another, as is the case with the building ensembles at both ends of the bridge spanning between Vasastaden and Kungsholmen on St. Eriksgatan.

In the immediate vicinity of the Karolinska Institute, which annually determines the winner of the Nobel Prize in Physiology or Medicine, Hagastaden is currently Stockholm's largest urban development area comprising 96 hectares, about three times the size of the famous old town. By 2030, around 50 000 workplaces and 6000 new apartments are to be created here, 3000 on the Stockholm side and 3000 in the subdistrict of Solna. Norra Tornen is therefore not only situated at the transition of two districts but also of two municipalities, without this being noticeable on the spot. The E4/E20 freeway and the Värtabanan railroad line have been tunneled and built over for this urban development project over a length of around 800 m.

Die Doppeltürme Norra Tornen, die „nördlichen Türme", stehen am Übergang von Vasastaden, einem Stadtteil mit Wohnbebauung überwiegend aus den 1930er Jahren, zum gerade neu entstehenden Stadtteil Hagastaden und bilden links und rechts der Ausfallstraße Torsgatan eine Torsituation aus. Das Motiv der Doppelturm-Tore markiert im Stadtbild Stockholms traditionell wichtige Punkte, etwa den Übergang von einer Insel zur nächsten, wie im Falle des Gebäudeensembles an beiden Enden der Brücke zwischen Vasastaden und Kungsholmen auf der St. Eriksgatan.

In direkter Nachbarschaft zum Karolinska Institut, das jährlich den Träger des Nobelpreises für Physiologie oder Medizin bestimmt, ist Hagastaden mit 96 Hektar Stockholms derzeit größtes Stadtentwicklungsgebiet und damit etwa dreimal so groß wie die berühmte Altstadt. Bis 2030 entstehen hier rund 50 000 Arbeitsplätze und 6000 neue Wohnungen, 3000 auf der Stockholmer Seite und 3000 auf der Gemarkung der Gemeinde Solna. Norra Tornen steht also nicht nur am Übergang von zwei Stadtteilen, sondern auch von zwei Kommunen, ohne dass dies vor Ort zu spüren wäre. Die Autobahn E4/E20 und die Bahnstrecke Värtabanan wurden für das Stadtentwicklungsprojekt auf einer Länge von rund 800 Metern übertunnelt und bebaut.

A typical Stockholm gate situation on St. Eriksgatan.
Eine für Stockholm typische Torsituation auf der St. Eriksgatan.

Rendering of Hagastaden with the two new towers in the north of Stockholm.
Rendering von Hagastaden mit den beiden neuen Türmen im Norden Stockholms.

The new Hagastaden district under construction.
Der neue Stadtteil Hagastaden im Bau.

Norra Tornen marks the transition to the new district and clearly represents a contemporary and sustainable vision for the city. At the same time, the towers are able to incorporate Stockholm's older architectural structure in their color scheme and rising shape. This mediation between the old and the new is one of the great design strengths of the project.

As you walk around the two towers called Innovationen and Helix, it becomes clear how small their footprints are. One downside is that the public spaces at the foot of the two towers have (as yet) received too little creative attention and their sojourn quality leaves a lot to be desired. All of a sudden, the towers come upon the square without a podium or plinth zone, as if they had been put down there.

The specification of already defined heights and contours of the outer shape ran the risk of transferring these parameters too directly into the architectural form. OMA broke away from the strict specifications of the planning authority by placing the main focus on the large number of balcony and terrace areas. The predetermined vertical structure and stepped form was balanced by the horizontal dissolution into cubes or pixels. The sheltered balconies and the cube-like modules alternate in a regular pattern and create a brutalist game of deception.

The ribbed structure and coloration of the precast concrete elements were analyzed in many tests. Some versions envisaged uncolored concrete or a manually chipped, rough, and jagged rib surface in the style of the design models of 1960s brutalism such as Paul Rudolph's Art + Architecture Building at Yale University in New Haven. With the soft brown of the implemented solution, the façade blends in perfectly with Stockholm's earthy color range, which includes all shades from beige to red. The ribs have been straightened with smooth cuts, which makes the admixed colorful pebbles stand out more clearly, an effect similar to that of a terrazzo floor. The cuts create a surprisingly velvety-smooth and very tactile surface, and the pebbles make the towers sparkle promisingly when they reflect the sun.

Norra Tornen markiert eindeutig den Übergang in den neuen Stadtteil und verkörpert eindeutig eine zeitgemäße und zukunftsfähige Vision für die Stadt. Gleichzeitig vermögen die Türme die ältere bauliche Struktur Stockholms in ihrer Farbigkeit und anwachsenden Figur aufzunehmen. Diese Vermittlung zwischen Alt und Neu ist eine der großen gestalterischen Stärken des Projekts.

Beim Umrunden der beiden Türme Innovationen und Helix wird deutlich, wie klein ihre Grundfläche ist. Ein Wermutstropfen ist, dass die öffentlichen Plätze am Fuße der beiden Türme (noch) zu wenig gestalterische Zuwendung erfahren haben und ihre Aufenthaltsqualität zu wünschen übrig lässt. Unvermittelt treffen die Türme ohne Podest oder Sockelzone auf den Platz, als wären sie dort abgestellt worden.

Die Vorgabe bereits festgelegter Höhen und des Umrisses der äußeren Form barg die Gefahr, diese Parameter zu direkt in die architektonische Gestalt zu übernehmen. OMA löste sich von den engen Vorgaben des Planungsamtes, indem sie das Hauptaugenmerk auf die Vielzahl von Balkon- und Terrassenflächen legten. Die vorgegebene vertikale Gliederung und getreppte Form wurde durch die horizontale Auflösung in Kuben bzw. Pixel ins Gleichgewicht gebracht. Die geschützten Balkone und die würfelartigen Module wechseln sich in regelmäßigem Muster ab und schaffen ein brutalistisches Vexierspiel.

Die Rippenstruktur und die Farbigkeit der Betonfertigteile wurden in vielen Versuchen analysiert. Einige Versionen sahen ungefärbten Beton vor oder eine handwerklich abgeschlagene, raue und zerklüftete Oberfläche der Rippen in Anlehnung an die gestalterischen Vorbilder des Brutalismus der 1960er Jahre, wie zum Beispiel Paul Rudolphs Art + Architecture Building der Yale University in New Haven. Mit dem sanften Braun der umgesetzten Lösung fügt sich die Fassade in die erdige Farbpalette Stockholms, die alle Schattierungen von Beige bis Rot umfasst, bestens ein. Die Rippen wurden mit glatten Schnitten begradigt, was die zugeschlagenen bunten Kieselsteine klarer zur Geltung bringt, ein Effekt wie bei einem Terrazzoboden. Die Schnitte schaffen eine überraschend samtig-glatte und sehr haptische Oberfläche, und die Kieselsteine lassen die Türme verheißungsvoll glitzern, wenn sie die Sonne reflektieren.

The two towers at the crossing of Torsgatan and Norra Stationsgatan were realized time-delayed.
Die beiden Türme an der Kreuzung Torsgatan / Norra Stationsgatan wurden zeitversetzt realisiert.

The small public square at the foot of the towers unfortunately offers little sjourn quality.
Der kleine öffentliche Platz am Fuß der Türme bietet leider wenig Aufenthaltsqualität.

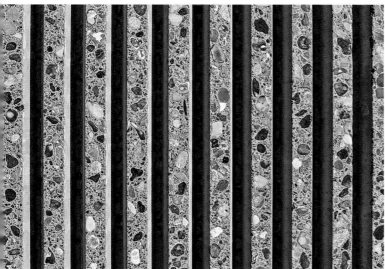

Detail of the ribbed structure of the façade
Detail der Rippenstruktur der Fassade

Paul Rudolph – Art & Architecture Building, Yale, 1961-63

The use of prefabricated façade elements made it possible to continue the construction work even at temperatures below 5 °C, when pouring concrete on site would no longer be possible. In addition, prefabrication saved considerable time — one story was completed in one week — and costs, which made the differentiated façade treatment and dynamic surface with its numerous recesses and projections economically feasible in the first place.

All apartments feature at least one balcony and are usually oriented in several directions. Even during Sweden's long, dark winter months, huge window areas bring the little remaining daylight into the interior. The view from the floor-to-ceiling windows and from the balconies with their glass parapets is almost dizzying.

The number and type of amenities available to all residents in the Innovationen highrise are generous by European standards but would probably not be adequate in New York. By means of an app, residents can book the cinema room for up to ten people, a small apartment for guests or the meeting room, which is equipped with a kitchen and offers space for larger dinner parties. A sauna, a small gym and a yoga room are available at any time. On the ground floor, both towers accommodate commercial areas. In the Helix tower, a public restaurant is to be set up on the roof terrace on the 16th floor.

Die vorgefertigten Fassadenelemente erlaubten es, die Bauarbeiten auch bei unter 5 °C fortzusetzen, wenn das Gießen von Ortbeton schon nicht mehr möglich wäre. Außerdem sparte die Vorfertigung erheblich Zeit – pro Woche wurde ein Stockwerk fertiggestellt – und Kosten, was die differenzierte Fassadenbehandlung und bewegte Oberfläche mit den zahlreichen Rück- und Vorsprüngen wirtschaftlich gesehen überhaupt erst möglich machte.

Alle Wohnungen haben mindestens einen Balkon und orientieren sich in der Regel in mehrere Richtungen. Riesige Fensterflächen bringen auch während Schwedens langer, dunkler Wintermonate das wenige Tageslicht ins Innere. Der Blick aus den bodentiefen Fenstern und von den Balkonen mit ihrer gläsernen Brüstung ist geradezu schwindelerregend.

Anzahl und Art der für alle Bewohner zugänglichen Aufenthaltsräume (in den USA amenities genannt) im Turm Innovationen sind für europäische Verhältnisse großzügig bemessen, für New York würden sie wohl nicht genügen. Mittels einer App können die Bewohner den Kinoraum für bis zu zehn Personen buchen, ferner ein kleines Apartment für Gäste oder den Versammlungsraum, der mit einer Küche ausgestattet ist und Platz für größere Dinnerpartys bietet. Eine Sauna, ein kleines Fitnessstudio und ein Yoga-Raum sind jederzeit verfügbar. Im Erdgeschoss der beiden Türme sind Gewerbeflächen untergebracht. Im Turm Helix soll eine öffentliche Gastronomie auf der Dachterrasse im 16. Stock eingerichtet werden.

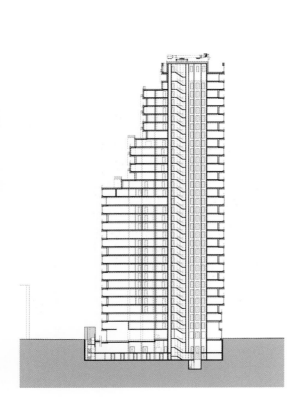

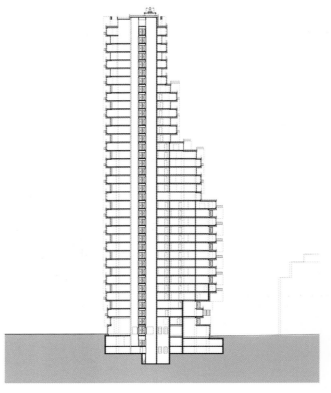

Long section
Längsschnitt

Innovationen Tower, 5th, 7th, 9th,
11th, 13th floor plan
Grundriss 5., 7., 9., 11., 13.
Obergeschoss

Innovationen Tower, 29th floor plan
Grundriss 29. Obergeschoss

Innovationen Tower, 30th + 32nd
floor plan
Grundriss 30. + 32. Obergeschoss

Reinier de Graaf in Conversation with Peter Cachola Schmal, Video-call, June 2020

Peter Cachola Schmal: Mr. de Graaf, are you still working from your home office?
Reinier de Graaf: Today I'm at home. I work partly from home. We have alternating shifts. In the Netherlands, we are allowed to have only a limited number of people in the office at the moment. I go to the office three days a week; two days of the week I work from home. And I've discovered that working remotely is quite effective in certain cases. When all of this is over, I will probably not travel as much as I used to, because I think there was a certain amount of unnecessary travel. You can have meetings via the screen that are equally productive. It's just the creative process, when you design, when you make models, when you walk around, when you look at things with the design team, that really needs physical presence.

PCS: With the TVCC (Television Cultural Center) in 2008, De Rotterdam in 2014, and the MahaNakhon in 2018, OMA was a finalist for the International Highrise Award three times but never won it. Until now.
RdG: I'm very happy we made it this time.

PCS: We were quite taken with the Norra Tornen. In a previous interview you called it a "*Plattenbau* for the rich."
RdG: That's the tagline, yes. To be honest, this was a name I gave it later. We won the competition in 2012. In 2014, I wrote an essay for *Baukultur in Deutschland: Von der Architekturqualität im Alltag zu den Ikonen der Baukunst* [published by Wüstenrot Stiftung]. They wanted me to write an essay about building culture in Germany. I chose to write about the *Plattenbau* in the former East Germany as a kind of tongue-in-cheek twist of fate, because it was something that had been discarded as building culture in Germany and was being demolished. The essay is also part of my book *Four Walls and a Roof*.
As the building in Stockholm is entirely prefabricated from the sixth floor up – floors, walls, and façade elements –, I saw that analogy and thought it was also a very good selling point. One of the things I learned when doing the research for the essay was that a lot of the parts, a lot of the panels, were actually produced in Finland, and some in France, on the other side of the Iron Curtain, where one can also find *Plattenbau*. I thought it was quite nice that the technique survived the political system it's most commonly associated with, and that the technique apparently survives any notion of class struggle. It was a tongue-in-cheek name, but people picked it up and it started to lead a life of its own.

PCS: It is very catchy. And is it really a building for the rich?
RdG: I have the distinct impression whenever I go to Sweden – I'm from the Netherlands – that almost everyone is well off. It's a country that seems to be doing pretty well. In Norra Tornen, apartment prices vary. Presumably, the penthouse is very expensive, but there are also a lot of smaller and more reasonable apartments. So, I don't think it's per se

Reinier de Graaf im Gespräch mit Peter Cachola Schmal, Videotelefonat, Juni 2020

Peter Cachola Schmal: Herr de Graaf, arbeiten Sie noch immer im Homeoffice?
Reinier de Graaf: Heute bin ich zuhause. Ich arbeite teilweise hier, wir haben wechselnde Schichten. In den Niederlanden darf sich aktuell nur eine begrenzte Anzahl von Personen im Büro aufhalten. Dreimal die Woche gehe ich dorthin; an zwei Tagen arbeite ich zuhause. Ich habe festgestellt, dass es in manchen Fällen sehr effektiv ist, aus der Ferne zu arbeiten. Wenn all das vorbei ist, werde ich vermutlich nicht mehr so viele Reisen unternehmen wie vorher; meiner Meinung nach waren sie zum Teil unnötig. Besprechungen via Bildschirm können genauso produktiv sein. Physische Präsenz ist nur im kreativen Prozess erforderlich – wenn man entwirft, Modelle baut, herumgeht und mit dem Entwurfsteam Dinge betrachtet.

PCS: Mit den Projekten TVCC (Television Cultural Center) in 2008, De Rotterdam in 2014 und MahaNakhon in 2018 wurde OMA dreimal für den Internationalen Hochhaus Preis nominiert, ohne ihn jedoch zu gewinnen. Bis jetzt.
RdG: Ich freue mich sehr, dass wir es diesmal geschafft haben.

PCS: Wir waren sehr beeindruckt von den Norra Tornen. In einem früheren Interview haben Sie das Projekt als „Plattenbau für Reiche" bezeichnet.
RdG: Ja, so lautet der Slogan, den ich dem Projekt ehrlich gesagt erst gegeben habe, nachdem wir den Wettbewerb 2012 gewonnen hatten. 2014 wurde ich gebeten, einen Essay zur Publikation *Baukultur in Deutschland: Von der Architekturqualität im Alltag zu den Ikonen der Baukunst* [herausgegeben von der Wüstenrot Stiftung] beizusteuern. Ich entschied mich, über den Plattenbau in der ehemaligen DDR als ironische Wendung des Schicksals zu schreiben, denn Plattenbauten wurden in Deutschland nicht länger als Baukultur angesehen und abgerissen. Der Essay ist auch in meinem Buch *Four Walls and a Roof* abgedruckt.
Die Analogie zum Plattenbau kam mir in den Sinn, weil das Gebäude in Stockholm von der sechsten Etage an komplett vorgefertigt ist – Böden, Wände und Fassadenelemente –, und ich hielt den Spruch für ziemlich werbewirksam. Im Zuge meiner Recherchen für den Essay habe ich herausgefunden, dass viele Bauelemente, viele Platten, seinerzeit in Finnland hergestellt wurden, einige auch in Frankreich – also diesseits des ehemaligen Eisernen Vorhangs, wo man ebenfalls Plattenbauten findet. Mir gefiel der Gedanke, dass die Plattenbauweise das politische System, mit dem sie am häufigsten in Verbindung gebracht wird, überlebt hat und offensichtlich über jede Art Klassenkampf erhaben ist. Mein Spruch war nicht ganz ernst gemeint, aber die Leute haben ihn aufgegriffen, und er begann ein Eigenleben zu führen.

PCS: Der Slogan ist auf jeden Fall eingängig. Ist es denn wirklich ein Gebäude für die Reichen?
RdG: Immer, wenn ich nach Schweden komme, habe ich als Niederländer den Eindruck, dass die meisten Menschen dort recht wohlhabend sind. Diesem Land scheint es ziemlich gut zu gehen. In den Norra Tornen variieren die Wohnungspreise. Das Penthouse ist

Despite their individual appearance, the towers consist of standardized and prefabricated elements that were mounted on the construction site, similar to classic prefabricated buildings.
Trotz individuellem Erscheinungsbild bestehen die Türme ähnlich wie klassische Plattenbauten aus standardisierten und vorgefertigten Elementen, die auf der Baustelle zusammengefügt wurden.

for the rich. It's not a luxury project, and I also don't like to think of it as a luxury project. I like to think of it as a residential building.

PCS: What are the advantages of using a prefabricated construction system?
RdG: The prefabricated system we used for Norra Tornen has the advantage that construction could carry on throughout the entire year, including the winter months, when pouring in-situ concrete would be difficult and is very costly. From a design point of view, prefabrication allowed us to achieve maximum variation with the least number of details, which again was more economical compared to traditional construction methods. As such, Norra Tornen can serve as a model for other projects.

PCS: What does the recurrence of a *Plattenbau* mean to you personally?
RdG: I grew up in a *Plattenbau*. When we had relatives visiting us, they would often comment that the anonymous and repetitive apartment buildings were disconcerting. But I was quite happy there. There was a sense of familiarity. To me and my parents the equality of the buildings was reflecting the equality of their inhabitants.

PCS: Has the developer sold all the apartments in Norra Tornen?
RdG: At least in the Innovationen tower. There are some units left for sale in the second tower, Helix. It's a nice location. And the apartments are nice, too. I don't know how COVID-19 has affected the whole thing, but I think it sold well.

PCS: Is your client still involved in operating the building?
RdG: Yes, Oscar Properties are still involved and they are very hands-on and good to work with. The Helix tower, however, is being managed by another developer.

PCS: Is it one person that represents the client or is it a board that you work with?
RdG: The client is Oscar Properties, and I mostly work with Oscar Engelbert (CEO and founder). I have a very direct contact with him. The real estate company bears his name, and he's really the face of it. That has been quite pleasant. I never have to go through an entire board, and votes, et cetera. We discussed the design with him, he liked it, and then he went for it. There are certain benefits to this type of leadership.

PCS: What sort of developer is he or his firm? What does he stand for?
RdG: He's a young developer. He does a lot of residential projects and also many conversions of older buildings into modern residential buildings. He's part of a young modern breed of developers, a post-Donald Trump type of developer, for whom not just Excel sheets and profits count, but also social issues, recyclability, sustainability, and actually architectural quality. That's how I would describe him. I have a couple of clients like him, younger property developers, who of course need to make money, but they're not motivated exclusively by it. These guys are a lot less cut-throat than the previous generations.

vermutlich sehr teuer, aber es gibt auch viele kleinere und günstigere Wohnungen. Ich würde also nicht per se sagen, dass es ein Gebäude für die Reichen ist. Es ist kein Luxusprojekt – zudem gefällt mir diese Betrachtungsweise auch nicht. Ich sehe es lieber als Wohngebäude.

PCS: Welche Vorteile ergeben sich aus dem Einsatz vorgefertigter Bauteile?
RdG: Im Falle der Norra Tornen konnten die Bauarbeiten dadurch das ganze Jahr über fortgesetzt werden – selbst in den Wintermonaten, in denen das Gießen von Ortbeton schwierig und kostspielig geworden wäre. Aus gestalterischer Sicht hat uns die Vorfertigung maximale Variationsmöglichkeit bei geringstmöglicher Anzahl von Details eröffnet – was im Vergleich zu traditionellen Bauweisen wiederum viel wirtschaftlicher war. Insofern kann das Projekt Norra Tornen als Vorbild für andere Projekte dienen.

PCS: Welche Bedeutung hat es für Sie persönlich, die Idee des Plattenbaus fortzuführen?
RdG: Ich bin in einem Plattenbau aufgewachsen. Auf Verwandte, die uns besuchten, wirkten die anonymen, gleichförmigen Wohnblöcke oftmals befremdlich. Ich war dort allerdings sehr glücklich. Es herrschte ein Gefühl der Vertrautheit. Für meine Eltern und mich spiegelte sich in der Gleichheit dieser Gebäude die Gleichheit ihrer Bewohner wider.

PCS: Konnte der Projektentwickler alle Wohnungen in den Norra Tornen verkaufen?
RdG: Zumindest im Turm Innovationen. Im zweiten Hochhaus, Helix, stehen noch einige Wohnungen zum Verkauf. Die Lage ist schön – die Wohnungen sind es ebenso. Ich weiß nicht, wie sich COVID-19 auf das Projekt insgesamt ausgewirkt hat, aber ich würde sagen, die Wohnungen haben sich gut verkauft.

PCS: Ist der Bauherr noch am Betrieb des Gebäudes beteiligt?
RdG: Ja, Oscar Properties sind noch immer involviert. Sie sind sehr pragmatisch und angenehm in der Zusammenarbeit. Der Turm Helix wird allerdings von einem anderen Bauträger betreut.

PCS: Wird Ihr Bauherr von einer Person vertreten, oder arbeiten Sie mit einem Vorstand zusammen?
RdG: Der Bauherr ist Oscar Properties, und ich arbeite hauptsächlich mit Oscar Engelbert, dem CEO und Gründer, zusammen. Wir stehen in direktem Kontakt. Die Immobiliengesellschaft trägt seinen Namen, und er ist auch das Gesicht des Unternehmens. Das macht die Zusammenarbeit sehr angenehm. Ich muss mich nie durch ein ganzes Gremium arbeiten, durch Abstimmungen et cetera. Wir diskutierten den Entwurf mit ihm, er gefiel ihm und dann setzten wir ihn um. Diese Art der Unternehmensführung hat einige Vorteile.

PCS: Wie würden Sie ihn als Projektentwickler beziehungsweise sein Unternehmen charakterisieren? Wofür steht Oscar Engelbert?
RdG: Er ist ein junger Projektentwickler. Er realisiert zahlreiche Wohnungsprojekte und Umwandlungen älterer Gebäude in moderne Wohnanlagen. Er gehört zu einer modernen Generation von Bauträgern, vom Typus Post-Donald-Trump, für die nicht nur Excel-Tabellen und Profite zählen, sondern auch soziale

View into the illuminated lobby of Innovationen
Blick in die beleuchtete Eingangshalle von Innovationen

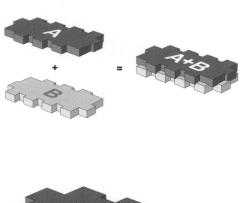

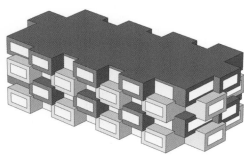

The use of prefabricated elements enabled rapid construction progress on a relatively small construction si
Der Einsatz von vorgefertigten Elementen ermöglichte einen zügigen Baufortschritt auf einer relativ kleinen Baustelle

PCS: That sounds like he is an interesting partner to work with. The beginning of the project was an international competition that you won, right?
RdG: I don't remember how international the competition was, to be honest. I think Wingårdhs was part of the competition and three or four other parties. Each pitched for the project with their own developer. We presented the project to the municipality a number of times, took in their comments, and then we were awarded it.

The project started with two envelopes drawn on the site by the city architect [Aleksander Wolodarski], who had meanwhile retired, but the envelopes, which looked like two church pipe organs standing up straight, had been fixed in the binding local plan. Therefore, we had to operate carefully not to break that envelope. However, we didn't like the envelope; we didn't like the style or the aesthetics that it suggested. So, we took the envelope, left the even floors as they were, and flipped the odd floors. In this way the design resulted in a kind of pixel system and made it look completely different than the initially prescribed envelope, while at the same time completely respecting it. Therefore, we didn't have to go through the whole procedure of getting permits again. The form is partly a result of a manipulation of something that was given, then we standardized it and turned it into this hammered concrete system.

PCS: It reminds me of structuralism of the 1960s and 1970s, especially of Moshe Safdie's Habitat 67 in Montreal, Canada.
RdG: It's a big compliment, because that's a very beautiful project. I think this is still a very interesting period. It's been a period that has been ignored for a long time but that is increasingly rediscovered. I wrote a lot about it in my book *Four Walls and a Roof*.

PCS: For Stockholm the project is quite high – currently the highest building in the city – and of course quite different from its surroundings. In spite of that, and beyond the immediate physical, how does it relate to a larger political, societal, or economic context?
RdG: First of all, the composition of twin towers flanking a major thoroughfare is not new in Stockholm. Take for example the Kungstornen built in the 1920s. Moreover, Norra Tornen is located at a traffic intersection, which merits a special approach to both design and building height. But again, these were the givens from the city's urban planning department.

PCS: In your book *Four Walls and a Roof* you wrote a chapter about *The Box* mentioning that "the box is where architecture stops being a matter of individual creation" and that "only one in 12 487 boxes has the hope of being a beautiful box". How does this apply to the stacked boxes of Norra Tornen?
RdG: Norra Tornen is many boxes, so maybe we maximized the chance.

PCS: When will the second tower be completed?
RdG: This year. We watch the construction process on a webcam. At a certain time, in the case of the first tower, every six days a floor was completed. It

Fragen, Wiederverwertbarkeit, Nachhaltigkeit und die Qualität der Architektur. So würde ich ihn beschreiben. Ich habe mit einer Reihe solcher Bauherren wie ihm zu tun, jüngere Bauträger, die natürlich Geld verdienen müssen, aber ihre Motivation nicht nur daraus beziehen. Sie sind längst nicht so knallhart und gewinnorientiert wie vorherige Generationen.

PCS: Das klingt ganz danach, als sei Oscar Engelbert ein interessanter Geschäftspartner. Dem Projekt ging ein internationaler Wettbewerb voraus, den Sie für sich entscheiden konnten, richtig?
RdG: Um ehrlich zu sein, erinnere ich mich nicht mehr daran, wie international der Wettbewerb war. Ich glaube, Wingårdhs war an diesem Wettbewerb beteiligt sowie drei oder vier andere Büros. Jedes Büro hat mit seinem eigenen Projektentwickler teilgenommen. Wir präsentierten das Projekt der Stadtverwaltung mehrmals, nahmen ihre Kommentare auf und erhielten schließlich den Zuschlag.
Der Ausgangspunkt des Projekts waren zwei Gebäudeumrisse, die der damalige Stadtarchitekt [Aleksander Wolodarski] für den Ort entworfen hatte. Sie glichen aufrecht stehenden Orgelpfeifen und waren im verbindlichen Bebauungsplan festgeschrieben worden. Wir mussten also behutsam vorgehen, um diese Hülle nicht zu verletzen. Allerdings gefiel sie uns nicht gerade – weder ihr Stil noch ihre Ästhetik, die sie nahelegte. Also nahmen wir diese äußere Form, behielten die geraden Geschosse wie geplant bei, verschoben jedoch die ungeraden Geschosse. Auf diese Weise ergab sich eine Art Pixelsystem, ein Design, das gänzlich anders aussieht als die ursprünglich vorgeschriebene Hülle, diese aber gleichzeitig vollkommen respektiert. Deshalb mussten wir das Genehmigungsverfahren nicht erneut durchlaufen. Die Form resultiert zum Teil aus einer Veränderung der Vorgaben, das Ergebnis hiervon haben wir dann standardisiert und in das System aus geriffeltem Beton übersetzt.

PCS: Das Projekt erinnert mich an den Strukturalismus der 1960er und 1970er Jahre, insbesondere an Moshe Safdies Habitat 67 in Montreal, Kanada.
RdG: Das ist ein großes Kompliment, denn das ist ein wunderschönes Projekt. Ich finde diese Phase noch immer sehr interessant. Diese Zeit wurde lange Zeit übergangen, wird aber sukzessive wiederentdeckt. In meinem Buch *Four Walls and a Roof* habe ich einiges über diese Phase geschrieben.

PCS: Für Stockholmer Verhältnisse ist das Projekt recht hoch – das derzeit höchste Gebäude der Stadt – und unterscheidet sich natürlich deutlich von seiner Umgebung. Abgesehen von der Höhe und dem unmittelbaren physischen Umfeld: Wie positioniert sich der Bau im größeren politischen, gesellschaftlichen oder wirtschaftlichen Kontext?
RdG: Zunächst einmal ist die Komposition von Zwillingstürmen an einer Hauptverkehrsachse nicht neu für Stockholm. Nehmen Sie zum Beispiel die Kungstornen aus den 1920er Jahren. Außerdem befindet sich das Projekt Norra Tornen an einem (Verkehrs-)Knotenpunkt, weshalb es sowohl im Hinblick auf die Gestaltung als auch auf die Gebäudehöhe einen ganz besonderen Ansatz verdient. Aber wie gesagt, dies waren die Vorgaben der Stadtplanungsbehörde.

was progressing so fast. This is quite interesting, because the materials and the detailing are not cheap. They are actually quite sophisticated. But as a whole, the building is not extravagantly expensive, because whatever you spend on materials you earn back in construction time. And, of course, construction time, particularly in Western Europe, is a very big factor in the cost of buildings.

PCS: What sort of amenities or common facilities, compared to residential towers in America or Asia, can the owners of the apartments use?
RdG: There's a fitness studio in the basement of the tower. There's a shared lobby. But that's about it. It's not an Asian tower which has so many facilities that – in theory – you never have to leave the building. That's not the culture in Sweden. You have your neighborhoods there. Particularly in the center of the city you have all the things you need around the corner.

PCS: Do you have contact with anybody that has bought an apartment?
RdG: I did, but I haven't spoken to them in a long time.

PCS: What did they tell you? How do people feel in the building as residents?
RdG: When I spoke to them, and they knew my role in creating the building, they were always very nice to me, obviously. They seemed happy. They spoke of it fondly. I don't know whether that's the case for all of the residents. I haven't been to Sweden in quite some time, and COVID-19 might prevent me from doing so in the near future. I think it's actually a very nice building to self-isolate in, because you have such a terrific view. If Sweden had had very strict lockdown measures, the building would have been perfect.

PCS: Do people buy apartments as a means of investing money like they do in London?
RdG: No. The Swedish housing market was very good for some time, but it has fluctuated quite a bit. So I don't think you see what you have in Vancouver, for example, where property is an investment and stands empty. People in Sweden buy apartments or houses to live in them.

PCS: In Sweden, you have severe winters, and therefore you need insulation to meet the energy saving rules. Compared to the *Plattenbau*, how much insulation material is inside the walls?
RdG: We used a sandwich panel system. The recessed balconies have sliding doors with insulated frames. Almost all windows are uninterrupted by transoms or mullions. Mullions are, even when insulated, always the weak parts in terms of energy efficiency. Therefore, we chose to use a single sheet of glass to improve the thermal qualities of the building. A *Plattenbau*, of course, is notoriously energy inefficient and notoriously noisy. In Eastern Europe, you had buildings planned to be completely prefabricated and then built from bricks. Even though they are supposedly more basic, this was the luxurious version. It is ironic that brick has outperformed the supposedly more sophisticated concrete paneling. But this is no longer the case in the 21st century.

PCS: In Ihrem Buch *Four Walls and a Roof* schreiben Sie im Kapitel „The Box", dass die Box dort sei, wo die Architektur aufhöre, Gegenstand der individuellen Schöpfung zu sein, und dass bei nur einer von 12 487 Boxen die Hoffnung bestehe, dass sie eine schöne Box ist. Wie passt das zu den gestapelten Boxen im Falle der Norra Tornen?
RdG: Die Norra Tornen sind viele Boxen, vielleicht haben wir somit die Chance maximiert.

PCS: Wann wird der zweite Turm fertiggestellt sein?
RdG: Dieses Jahr. Wir verfolgen den Bauprozess per Webcam. Beim Bau des ersten Turms wurde ab einem gewissen Zeitpunkt alle sechs Tage ein Stockwerk fertiggestellt. Der Bau schritt so schnell voran, was ziemlich interessant ist, denn die Materialien und die Detaillierung sind eigentlich recht anspruchsvoll und keineswegs günstig. Insgesamt ist das Gebäude jedoch nicht übermäßig teuer, denn was immer man in Materialien investiert, bekommt man an Bauzeit zurück. Und natürlich ist die Bauzeit ein immenser Kostenfaktor, insbesondere in Westeuropa.

PCS: Welche Aufenthaltsräume oder Gemeinschafts-einrichtungen – im Vergleich zu Wohnhochhäusern in Amerika oder Asien – stehen den Wohnungseigen-tümern zur Verfügung?
RdG: Im Untergeschoss des Turms Innovationen ist ein Fitnessstudio untergebracht und es gibt eine gemein-same Lobby, aber das war's auch schon. Es ist kein asiatischer Turm, der so viele Funktionen und Dienst-leistungen bietet, dass man das Gebäude – theoretisch – nie verlassen muss. Das passt nicht zur schwedischen Kultur. Dort hat man seinen Stadtteil, seinen Kiez. Vor allem im Zentrum der Stadt findet man alles, was man braucht, direkt um die Ecke.

PCS: Haben Sie Kontakt zu Wohnungseigentümern?
RdG: Ja, aber wir haben uns lange nicht mehr gesprochen.

PCS: Was haben sie Ihnen erzählt? Wie fühlen sie sich als Bewohner der Norra Tornen?
RdG: Wenn ich mit ihnen gesprochen habe und sie um meine Rolle bei der Entstehung des Gebäudes wussten, waren sie natürlich immer sehr nett zu mir. Sie schienen glücklich und sehr angetan. Ich weiß nicht, ob das bei allen Bewohnern der Fall ist. Ich war schon lange nicht mehr in Schweden, und wegen COVID-19 wird das in nächster Zukunft möglicherweise so bleiben. Ich halte es sogar für ein sehr schönes Gebäude, um sich darin zu isolieren, denn man hat eine absolut großartige Aussicht. Hätte Schweden einen strengen Lockdown erlebt, wäre das Gebäude perfekt gewesen.

PCS: Werden die Wohnungen auch als Investitions-objekte gekauft, wie in London?
RdG: Nein. Der schwedische Wohnungsmarkt war eine Zeitlang sehr stabil, unterlag jedoch einigen Schwan-kungen. Insofern glaube ich nicht, dass Sie das beobachten werden, was zum Beispiel in Vancouver der Fall ist, wo Immobilien als reine Investition betrachtet werden und leer stehen. Die Menschen in Schweden kaufen Wohnungen oder Häuser, um darin zu wohnen.

PCS: In Schweden sind die Winter streng und es bedarf einer Isolierung, um die Energiesparvorschriften zu erfüllen. Wie viel Dämmmaterial, verglichen mit Platten-

Staggered play of the prefabricated concrete moduls
Gestaffeltes Spiel der vorfabrizierten Betonelemente

PCS: I read that the exposed gravel in the concrete should let it look like bricks. Why not just use bricks then?

RdG: The brown of the façade is a contextual reference to the color of Stockholm's buildings, not literally to their material. Besides, made of brick, Norra Tornen would not have been a "*Plattenbau* for the rich".

PCS: How do the balconies and the concrete perform in the very severe Swedish winters? If they still have severe winters, that is.

RdG: What I like is that there is a culture of balconies in Scandinavia even though the winters can be severe. In winter you don't use it the way you use it in summer. You have the liberty to not use it. If you look at Russia, they had a law in Soviet times that every apartment should have a balcony. But the first thing people did was to close them and use the area as storage space. Obviously, that would be quite difficult to do with the balconies in Norra Tornen.

Another interesting thing about Norra Tornen is that the rooms with the large, uninterrupted sheet of glass, which is not operable, are ventilated through the concrete ribs. The ribs are used to conceal an operable window lateral to the façade.

PCS: Is it like forced ventilation that is always on?

RdG: No. It's an operable part that can be opened. It's like ventilating a room in a normal housing unit, except you don't see it. There are certain ribs that are open. We built one apartment on site before the construction of the tower started, and tested many concrete panels. We tested all the details until they were absolutely right. There was a lot of back and forth, looking, trying, checking. Then once it worked, the construction company could roll out the thing without us. You could say we had a kind of mini villa on a nearby site that was our construction site before there was a proper construction site, where we tested everything extensively. It was a very pleasant collaboration with the client. He knew how important the detailing was, and no energy or money was spared on working on this mockup. A lot of clients would say that a mockup is expensive and decide against it.

PCS: If he was going to reproduce it a thousand times, then he'd better do it right.

RdG: I can guarantee you that there are a lot of clients that reproduce elements a thousand times without feeling any urge to test them. While we consider this is a normal thing to do, it's less common than you might think.

PCS: So, are there any plans to continue the collaboration in the future?

RdG: I think fondly of the client, and I can only hope he thinks the same of us. Maybe this award will help continue the collaboration.

bauten, befindet sich in den Wänden?

RdG: Wir haben ein Sandwichpaneel-System verwendet. Die zurückversetzten Balkone haben Schiebetüren mit isolierten Rahmen. Nahezu alle Fenster wurden ohne Fensterkreuze geplant. Pfosten stellen, auch wenn sie isoliert sind, in Bezug auf die Energieeffizienz immer eine Schwachstelle dar. Deshalb haben wir uns für die Verwendung einer durchgehenden Glasscheibe entschieden, um die thermischen Eigenschaften des Gebäudes zu verbessern. Der Plattenbau ist bekanntermaßen energieineffizient und laut. In Osteuropa wurden Gebäude komplett vorgefertigt geplant, dann aber doch aus Ziegelsteinen erstellt. Obwohl Ziegelbauten als einfacher gelten, war das die Luxusvariante. Es ist paradox, dass Ziegel die vermeintlich anspruchsvollere Betonverkleidung übertroffen haben. Im 21. Jahrhundert ist dies jedoch nicht mehr der Fall.

PCS: Ich habe gelesen, dass der sichtbare Kies den Beton wie Ziegel aussehen lassen sollten. Warum dann nicht gleich Ziegel verwenden?

RdG: Das Braun der Fassade ist ein kontextueller Verweis auf die Farbe der Stockholmer Gebäude, nicht unmittelbar auf ihr Material. Außerdem wären die Norra Tornen in Backstein kein „Plattenbau für Reiche" gewesen.

PCS: Wie bewähren sich die Balkone und der Beton in den sehr strengen schwedischen Wintern? Falls es überhaupt noch strenge Winter gibt.

RdG: Mir gefällt, dass es in Skandinavien eine Balkonkultur gibt, auch wenn die Winter manchmal streng sind. Im Winter nutzt man sie anders als im Sommer. Und man hat die Freiheit, sie nicht zu benutzen. In Russland gab es zu Sowjetzeiten ein Gesetz, wonach jede Wohnung einen Balkon haben musste. Das Erste, was die Leute jedoch taten, war, sie zu schließen und als Lagerraum zu nutzen. Das wäre bei den Balkonen der Norra Tornen schwer zu bewerkstelligen.

Ein weiterer interessanter Aspekt der Norra Tornen ist, dass die Räume mit der großen durchgehenden Glasscheibe, die nicht geöffnet werden kann, durch offene Betonrippen belüftet werden. Diese Rippen verdecken ein öffenbares Fenster seitlich der Fassade.

PCS: Ist das eine Art ständige aktive Zwangsbelüftung?

RdG: Nein. Es handelt sich um ein bewegliches Teil, das geöffnet werden kann. Es ist mit der Raumbelüftung in einer normalen Wohneinheit vergleichbar, nur dass man das Fenster nicht sieht. Gewisse Rippen sind offen. Wir haben vor Ort eine Wohnung erstellt, bevor mit dem Bau des Turms begonnen wurde, und haben viele Betonelemente getestet. Sämtliche Details wurden so lange untersucht, bis sie perfekt waren. Es gab eine Menge Hin und Her, Begutachten, Ausprobieren, Prüfen. Als schließlich alles funktionierte, konnte die Baufirma die Sache ohne uns in Angriff nehmen. Man könnte sagen, wir hatten eine Art Mini-Villa auf einer Baustelle in der Nähe – unserer Baustelle, bevor es eine richtige Baustelle gab –, wo wir alles ausgiebig testen konnten. Die Zusammenarbeit mit Oscar Properties war sehr

The rib structure of the façade is particulary evident when viewed from below.
Die Rippenstruktur der Fassade kommt besonders in der Aufsicht zur Geltung.

Reinier de Graaf with a model of both towers
Reinier de Graaf mit einem Modell der beiden Türme

angenehm. Sie wussten, wie wichtig uns die Detailplanung ist, und es wurden keine Kosten und Mühen bei der Arbeit an diesem Mock-up gescheut. Viele Kunden halten einen Musterraum oder eine Musterfassade für zu teuer und entscheiden sich dagegen.

PCS: Wenn man etwas tausendfach reproduzieren möchte, sollte man es besser genau nehmen.
RdG: Ich kann Ihnen versichern, dass es viele Kunden gibt, die Elemente tausendfach reproduzieren, ohne den Drang zu verspüren, sie vorher zu testen. Auch wenn wir das Testen für normal halten, ist es weniger üblich, als Sie vielleicht denken.

PCS: Es gibt also Pläne, die Zusammenarbeit mit Oscar Properties künftig fortzusetzen?
RdG: Ich halte sehr viel von diesem Bauherrn und kann nur hoffen, dass er von uns dasselbe denkt. Vielleicht wird dieser Preis dazu beitragen, dass unsere Zusammenarbeit eine Fortsetzung erfährt.

Oscar Engelbert in Conversation with Peter Cachola Schmal, Stockholm, August 2020

Peter Cachola Schmal: Congratulations on the International Highrise Award 2020 and on the winning project Norra Tornen by OMA. This mock-up piece of the façade made of concrete is wonderful to touch. But the realized version is not exactly like this. What was wrong with this sample? Was it a lot of manual work?

Oscar Engelbert: No, this is one of many, many samples. No matter what we did, it was a lot of manual work. We were striving for perfection. And I think this sample was a bit too edgy. The final building is more brown, almost sandy.

PCS: Are the people, owners and residents happy with this brutalist concrete?

OE: Well, I think most of them are. Especially the owners are very happy with the building and the result of the architecture. I get a lot of positive feedback. People approach me because they love it. I get a lot of text messages or mails, like "I love what you do for Stockholm", and "these buildings are fantastic". But then you follow the social media feed and you see someone posting on Twitter, "this is the ugliest building I've ever seen in my life", or "how can we have this brutalist architecture in Stockholm, it is terrible". And on Instagram, you constantly get pictures from people who like the project and from those who don't like it.

That is a successful building to me – when some people hate it and some love it and there are different feelings about it. Because this is what should happen when you do something—especially in architecture. It's like looking at a piece of art. Some people love it and some people hate it. If we would live in a city where everything looks the same that would be boring. And I think in many cities or in some parts of Stockholm, a lot of new neighborhoods look exactly the same. In my opinion, a new development or a new neighborhood should consist of many different types of buildings to be interesting. It's the mix.

There are many things about social media I don't like, but I like these tags that you can follow up, because I can see what everybody writes about the project, and that's really great.

PCS: Norra Tornen is very unique. Stockholm is not a high-rise city, and now there is this gate of two towers standing out. Did you develop the idea of the gate yourself?

OE: No. The master plan was developed by Aleksander Wolodarski, an architect who worked for the city. But the architecture was very different; I did not like what he had done. Luckily, the city and the developer couldn't reach an agreement. The moment I saw this in the news, I instantly contacted the head of the city and kept calling every three or four weeks to see what was going on. Six or eight months later, they launched a competition where many developers got the opportunity to bid for the property. It was one of the first times in Stockholm that the department that owns the land and the planning and development department worked together. Therefore, the competition was not only about money, it was also about what the towers

Oscar Engelbert im Gespräch mit Peter Cachola Schmal, Stockholm, August 2020

Peter Cachola Schmal: Meinen Glückwunsch zum Internationalen Hochhaus Preis 2020 und zum Gewinnerprojekt Norra Tornen von OMA. Diese Muster-fassade aus Beton hat eine wunderbare Haptik, ent-spricht aber nicht ganz der realisierten Variante. Was sprach gegen dieses Muster? War der manuelle Arbeits-aufwand zu hoch?

Oscar Engelbert: Nein, das ist nur ein Muster unter sehr, sehr vielen. Egal, was wir taten – alles bedeutete enorm viel Handarbeit. Wir strebten nach Perfektion. Ich denke, dieses Muster war etwas zu ausgefallen. Das endgültige Gebäude ist eher braun, beinahe sandig.

PCS: Sind die Menschen, die Eigentümer und Bewoh-ner, glücklich mit dem brutalistischen Beton?

OE: Ich denke, die meisten schon. Vor allem die Eigentümer sind mit dem Gebäude und dem architek-tonischen Ergebnis sehr zufrieden. Ich bekomme viel positives Feedback. Die Leute kommen auf mich zu, weil sie das Gebäude mögen. Ich erhalte eine Menge Textnachrichten oder Mails mit Aussagen wie „Ich finde es großartig, was Sie für Stockholm tun" und „Diese Gebäude sind fantastisch". Aber dann folgt man den Feeds auf den sozialen Medien und jemand schreibt auf Twitter: „Das ist das hässlichste Gebäude, das ich in meinem ganzen Leben gesehen habe", oder: „Wie kann es solch eine brutalistische Architektur in Stockholm geben, das ist schrecklich." Und auf Instagram trifft man ständig auf Bilder von Leuten, denen das Projekt gefällt, oder von solchen, denen es nicht gefällt.

Das macht für mich ein erfolgreiches Gebäude aus – dass es von den einen gehasst und von den anderen geliebt wird, dass es unterschiedliche Gefühle hervorruft. Genau das sollte geschehen, wenn man etwas schafft – vor allem in der Architektur. Es ist, als würde man ein Kunstwerk betrachten. Manche Menschen lieben es, andere verabscheuen es. Würden wir in einer Stadt leben, in der alles gleich aussieht, wäre das langweilig. In vielen Städten oder in einigen Teilen Stockholms sieht meines Erachtens ein Großteil der neuen Stadtviertel genau gleich aus. Ich finde, eine neue Bebauung oder ein neues Stadtviertel muss aus vielen verschiedenen Gebäudetypen bestehen, um interessant zu sein. Die Mischung macht's.

Es gibt vieles, das mir an Social Media nicht gefällt, aber ich mag diese Tags, denen man folgen kann. Auf diese Weise sehe ich alles, was über das Projekt geschrieben wird, und das ist wirklich großartig.

PCS: Das Projekt Norra Tornen ist sehr besonders. Stockholm ist keine Hochhausstadt, und nun steht da dieses Tor aus zwei Türmen. Haben Sie diese Tor-Idee selbst entwickelt?

OE: Nein. Der Masterplan stammt von Aleksander Wolodarski, einem Architekten, der für die Stadt ge-arbeitet hat. Die Architektur war jedoch eine ganz andere; mir gefiel sein Entwurf nicht. Zum Glück konnten sich die Stadt und der Bauträger nicht einigen. Als ich das in den Nachrichten sah, kontaktierte ich sofort den Verantwortlichen bei der Stadt und rief alle drei bis vier Wochen an, um zu hören, was vor sich geht. Sechs bis acht Monate später wurde ein Wettbewerb ausgelobt, bei dem viele Bauträger die Möglichkeit bekamen, ein Angebot für das Grundstück abzugeben. Das war eines der ersten Male in Stockholm, dass die

The more than 300 apartments of Norra Tornen are part of the comprehensive Hagastaden master plan including 6000 units.

Die etwas über 300 Wohnungen von Norra Tornen sind Bestandteil der 6000 Wohnungen umfassenden Masterplan für Hagastaden.

Early concrete sample from the design process at the office of Oscar Properties.
Frühes Betonmuster aus dem Entwurfsprozess im Büro von Oscar Properties.

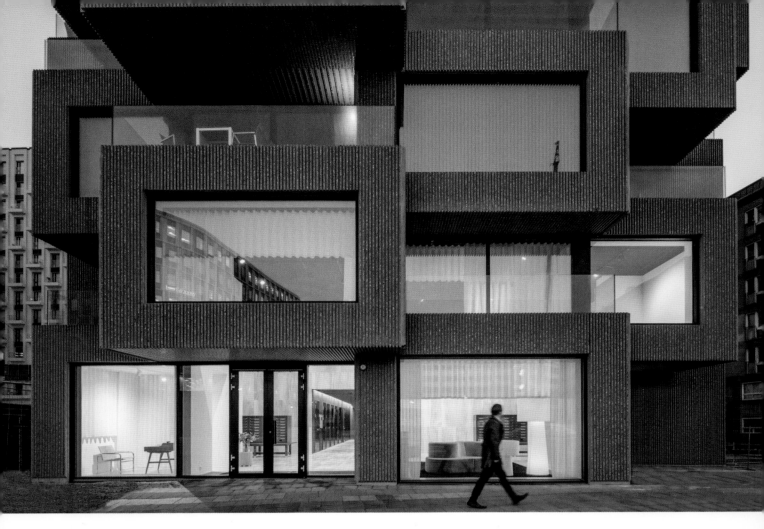

**Entrance situation and
lobby of Innovationen**
Eingangssituation und -halle
des Innovationen-Turms

should look like and what they would contribute to the city. For this reason, it was very clear to me who should be the architect. There have always been two architectural firms I wanted to work with: OMA and Herzog & de Meuron. We were already doing a project with Herzog & de Meuron, and for this particular site I thought OMA would be the right choice. Because they are very analytical about the way they look at each site and its difficulties and use architecture to solve the problem. The problem with this site was that the envelope was very small and the surrounding roads are very noisy. So, the architecture you see is an architecture that was based on solving the noise problem. And that's why you see all the balconies, so the sound wouldn't creep into the apartments.

PCS: Reinier de Graaf as the project architect told us how he further developed the given scheme. Whose idea was it that it should be a prefabricated brutalist building, which is not the first thing you think of nowadays?
OE: Of course OMA came up with the suggestion, and afterwards there was a lot of discussion about how to manufacture it and adjust the costs to achieve our targets. As in all cases, a good development is the result of the conversation between the developer and the architect.

PCS: We think that the Norra Tornen apartments are in the upper segment of the market. What is the standard price for these apartments per square meter?
OE: The average is about 11–12 000 euros per square meter. In the area around the towers, the average price today is 9500 euros. We are 15–20 percent above the average, which is still within reason. There is a range, of course. If you want to buy on the first ten floors, the price is anything from 8500 to 9800 euros. If you want to live on the top floor, it's going to cost more. If it wasn't for the fact that there are over 300 apartments, it would have been more expensive.

PCS: Interesting! What sorts of people buy these apartments?
OE: I stopped analyzing that. You just have to develop a great product. You have to stick to your feeling of what is good design and what is not. We have our own design team. So, everything you see in the apartments like kitchens, bathrooms, and floors has been designed by us. It is about finding the right balance to do something that is outstanding and really looks fantastic but also attracts a lot of buyers.

PCS: But your buyers are local, aren't they?
OE: Yeah, absolutely local.

PCS: There is no international investment, like we see it in Frankfurt?
OE: No. People buy apartments to live in them, which is good.

PCS: What kind of amenities do the buildings offer?
OE: In the first building, there is a gym, a sauna, a yoga space, a small cinema, a conference and dining room, and a small apartment for guests.

Grundstücksverwaltungsabteilung und die Planungs- und Entwick-lungsabteilung zusammengearbeitet haben. Bei diesem Wettbewerb spielten also nicht nur finanzielle Aspekte eine Rolle, es ging auch darum, wie die Türme aussehen sollten und welchen Beitrag sie für die Stadt leisten können. Deshalb war für mich klar, welches Architek-turbüro es sein sollte. Immer schon gab es zwei Büros, mit denen ich zusammenarbeiten wollte: OMA und Herzog & de Meuron. Wir arbeiteten bereits an einem Projekt mit Herzog & de Meuron, und bei diesem speziellen Standort hielt ich OMA für die richtige Wahl. Sie gehen nämlich sehr analytisch vor bei der Betrach-tung des jeweiligen Grundstücks und seiner Herausfor-derungen und nutzen Architektur, um Probleme zu lösen. Das Problem bei diesem Grundstück war, dass die Hülle sehr klein ist und die angrenzenden Straßen sehr laut sind. Die Architektur, die Sie hier sehen, basiert also auf der Lösung des Lärmproblems. Und daher rühren auch die Balkone: Sie sorgen dafür, dass der Lärm nicht in die Wohnungen dringt.

PCS: Der Projektarchitekt Reinier de Graaf hat uns erläutert, wie er das vorgegebene Schema weiter-entwickelt hat. Wessen Idee war dieser brutalistische Plattenbau? Das ist ja nicht gerade das Erste, woran man heute denkt.
OE: Der Vorschlag kam natürlich von OMA. Es folgte eine rege Diskussion darüber, wie man ihn umsetzen und die Kosten anpassen könnte, um unsere Ziele zu erreichen. Eine gute Umsetzung basiert stets auf dem Gespräch zwischen Projektentwickler und Architekten.

PCS: Wir vermuten, dass die Wohnungen in den Norra Tornen im oberen Marktsegment liegen. Wie hoch ist der übliche Kaufpreis pro Quadratmeter?
OE: Im Schnitt liegt er bei 11 000 bis 12 000 Euro pro Quadratmeter. Rund um die Türme beträgt der Preis heute durchschnittlich 9500 Euro. Wir sind also 15–20 Prozent teurer als der Durchschnitt, das liegt noch im Rahmen. Es gibt natürlich eine gewisse Preisspanne: Wenn man an einer Wohnung in den unteren zehn Stockwerken interessiert ist, liegt der Kaufpreis bei 8500 bis 9900 Euro. Wenn man in der obersten Etage wohnen möchten, ist das teurer. Gäbe es nicht mehr als 300 Wohnungen, wäre es noch teurer geworden.

PCS: Interessant! Was für Menschen kaufen diese Wohnungen?
OE: Ich habe aufgehört, das zu analysieren. Es gilt ein-fach, ein großartiges Produkt zu entwickeln. Man muss sich auf sein Gefühl verlassen, wenn es darum geht, was ein guter Entwurf ist und was nicht. Wir haben unser eigenes Entwurfsteam. Alles, was in den Wohnungen vorhanden ist, also Küchen, Badezimmer und Böden, wurde von uns entworfen. Es geht darum, das richtige Maß zu finden: ein Produkt zu entwerfen, das herausragt und fantastisch aussieht, aber auch eine breite Käuferschaft anspricht.

PCS: Aber Ihre Käuferschaft kommt aus der Umgebung, nicht wahr?
OE: Ja, absolut.

PCS: Es sind keine internationalen Investoren darunter, wie etwa in Frankfurt?
OE: Nein. Die Menschen kaufen die Wohnungen, um darin zu leben, und das ist gut so.

PCS: There are a few stores in it as well, right?
OE: Exactly. There is already a sunglasses store at Innovationen, the first tower. In the second one, Helix, we are aiming to have a deli, and we might have a restaurant on the 16th floor. So everyone will be able to see the building from inside and enjoy the view. But these COVID times are not the best time to find a restaurant that wants to expand and take this place. So, we have to think creatively and see what other things we can develop.

PCS: These buildings seem very well suited for someone who wants to work remotely on the own balcony in these times.
OE: Yes, that's right. And we were very lucky; in many countries construction just came to a halt. I didn't even want to think about the consequences of stopping construction works. I had to do it once, and it's really difficult to start construction after it has been stopped for six months. We were able to get the last deliveries from Italy before they locked down. We just shipped everything here, stored it, and so we were able to maintain construction during the whole lockdown.

PCS: Reinier de Graaf told us that you did a mock-up on site to test the prefabrication methods.
OE: Not a whole apartment, though. Well, in two different ways we did: there were mock-ups of the façade, we did like five, six or eight different versions. That's how we came to the conclusion what the façade should look like. But for internal purposes and for the sales office, we then created an apartment in a rented office space, where you had the kitchen, the bathroom and the balcony to see how it feels.

PCS: Are there any aspects of the prefabrication, which might come up again in other projects? Or are they really special, unique for this project?
OE: Personally, my mood right now is to develop buildings that are going to be competitive in the segment of rental apartments for people who don't really have the money, and to build them all over the country — and to use prefabrication because from the moment you start construction, the building is up in two to three months. I'm very interested in exploring good architecture combined with prefabrication, which can be produced so fast. This is something I am working on right now.
One floor took about one week to complete. The first five to six floors were made on site because there was a lot of concrete coming in to set up the base section. After that, it started to go faster. Eventually it was on average one floor per week, which was very fast. And then we used prefabricated bathrooms from Italy. They were just put in and that was it.
So, yes, to answer your question, there are many things to learn from. And I think prefabrication offers so many good opportunities.

PCS: We think of Scandinavian construction as being prefabricated wooden modules. Do you do that as well?
OE: We are working on one such project. Beside that, one idea that we explored earlier was to build the Gasklockan project in timber or in wood. But we

PCS: Welche Art von Serviceeinrichtungen bieten die Gebäude?
OE: Im Norra Tornen – Innovationen gibt es ein Fitness-studio, eine Sauna, einen Yoga-Bereich, ein kleines Kino, einen Konferenz- und Speiseraum sowie eine kleine Gästewohnung.

PCS: Zudem sind ein paar Läden vorgesehen.
OE: Ganz genau. Es gibt bereits ein Sonnenbrillen-geschäft in Innovationen, dem ersten Turm. Im Tower Helix planen wir ein Deli und gegebenenfalls ein Restaurant im 16. Stock. Auf diese Weise hätte jeder die Gelegenheit, das Gebäude von innen zu sehen und die Aussicht zu genießen. Aber diese COVID-19-Zeiten sind nicht der beste Zeitpunkt, um ein Restaurant zu finden, das expandieren und diesen Standort übernehmen möchte. Wir müssen also kreativ denken und schauen, welche Alternativen wir entwickeln können.

PCS: Diese Gebäude scheinen sich außerordentlich gut zu eignen für Menschen, die in diesen Zeiten von Zuhause aus, auf dem eigenen Balkon arbeiten möchten.
OE: Ja, richtig. Wir hatten auch großes Glück; in vielen Ländern kam der Bauprozess einfach zum Erliegen. Über die Folgen eines Baustopps wollte ich gar nicht erst nachdenken. Ich war einmal in dieser Situation und weiß, dass es wirklich schwierig ist, die Bauarbeiten fortzusetzen, wenn sie einmal ein halbes Jahr lang geruht haben. Wir hatten das Glück, die letzten Lieferungen aus Italien gerade noch zu erhalten, bevor dort der Lockdown kam. Wir haben einfach alles hierher liefern lassen und eingelagert. Auf diese Weise konnten wir die Bauarbeiten während des gesamten Lockdowns aufrechterhalten.

PCS: Reinier de Graaf hat uns erzählt, dass Sie anhand eines Musters die Vorfertigungsmethoden vor Ort erprobt haben.
OE: Allerdings war das keine ganze Musterwohnung. Wir sind auf zweierlei Arten vorgegangen: Es gab Musterfassaden, fünf, sechs oder acht verschiedene Versionen. So kamen wir zu dem Schluss, wie die Fassade aussehen sollte. Für interne Zwecke und für das Verkaufsbüro schufen wir dann eine Wohnung in einem gemieteten Büroraum: Dort konnte man die Küche, das Bad und den Balkon begutachten und einen Eindruck davon bekommen, wie sie wirken.

PCS: Gibt es Aspekte bei der Vorfertigung, die auf andere Projekte übertragbar wären? Oder sind sie wirklich nur speziell und einzig für dieses Projekt geeignet?
OE: Ich bin im Moment daran interessiert, Gebäude zu entwickeln, die im Mietwohnungssegment für Menschen, die sich das nicht wirklich leisten können, bestehen können; ich möchte sie im ganzen Land bauen – und zwar in Fertigbauweise, weil diese Gebäude zwei bis drei Monate nach Baubeginn bereits fertig sind. Ich habe ein großes Interesse daran, gute Architektur in Kombi-nation mit Vorfertigung zu entwickeln, die so schnell gebaut werden kann. Das ist eine Sache, an der ich gerade arbeite.
Die Fertigstellung einer Etage dauerte etwa eine Woche. Die ersten fünf bis sechs Stockwerke wurden vor Ort gebaut, da viel Beton für den Sockelbereich vonnöten war. Danach ging es zunehmend schneller. Schließlich lagen wir bei durchschnittlich einem Stockwerk pro

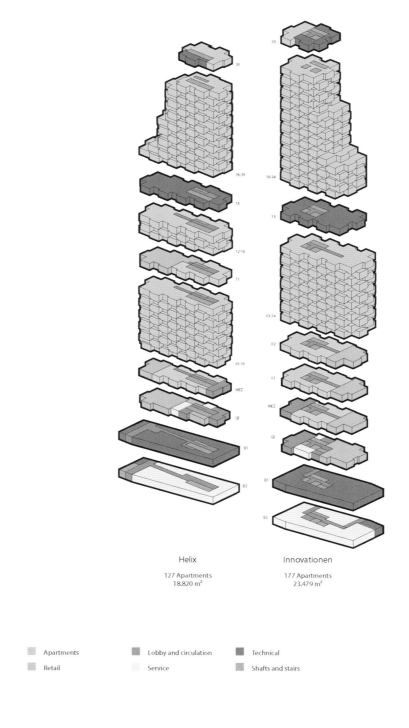

Helix

127 Apartments
18.820 m²

Innovationen

177 Apartments
23.479 m²

Apartments

Retail

Lobby and circulation

Service

Technical

Shafts and stairs

Distribution of apartments and uses
Wohnungs- und Nutzungsverteilung

79&Park in Stockholm by BIG – Bjarke Ingels Group was completed of prefabricated cubes in 2018.
79&Park in Stockholm von BIG – Bjarke Ingels Group wurde 2018 aus vorproduzierten Würfelelementen fertiggestellt.

For the H7 project which was completed in 2015 Oscar properties engaged six young practises to design six individual buildings.
Für das 2015 fertiggestellte Projekt H7 engagierten Oscar Properties sechs junge Architekturbüros um sechs individuelle Gebäude zu entwerfen.

couldn't make it happen, because using wood you can't build too high due to the fire risk. We couldn't find a way to prevent the wood from taking fire. Well, this was two years ago; now there is probably a way to do it.

PCS: Is there something about the project you would do differently today?
OE: Well, there is one thing I don't like. When you enter the lobby, there are two furniture elements for the mail boxes, which I don't like.

PCS: We see that the highrise movement in Europe is, of course, different from Asia and the US. Is there a highrise movement in Stockholm? Or is Norra Tornen seen as something very unique?
OE: We had a tower that we were going to build with Herzog & de Meuron. But then the City of Stockholm didn't want to decontaminate the land, a former gasometer site. And since we couldn't come to an agreement with the city, the project is now terminated, unfortunately. But it would have been our last contribution of a highrise to the city. I don't think there are many more places in Stockholm that are suitable for a highrise.

PCS: You have not only been working with Herzog & de Meuron on the Gasklockan tower, but also with BIG on a low-rise project. It looks like you prefer inter-national star architects. What do local architects think of that?
OE: We work with many young architects, too. The ones we haven't worked with are the medium and big-sized in between. We did a development in Hammarby sjöstad, for example. It was a very nice plot close to the water. However, my problem with the area was that most of the surrounding projects looked exactly the same, no difference, no variation. So, we bought a large site there for almost 200 apartments, and we did a competition for young architects who had just graduated, instead of going to the big star architects or the mid-sized firms. In the end, we completed those buildings in 2015 and created something totally new. Most of these architects still thank me for giving them the opportunity. We really enjoy working with young creative minds.

PCS: How would you describe yourself compared to the rest of the developers in the city?
OE: I think we have always been the upcoming developer, because the other developers have not liked us. Because we do something new. In Sweden, we had a housing shortage. We therefore created a new niche by buying commercial buildings and converting them for residential use. Beside that we did new developments. From 2012 to 2017 we grew from doing 112 apartments per year to 1500 apartments, which is significant. But we could only do so because the demand was there. It was a golden era for a lot of developers because prices were just going up. There were a lot of new developers coming up and bidding for land. As a consequence, land prices went up, and in parallel, it became more difficult to take out a loan to buy apartments. As a result, the demand, and therefore our operation, has decreased in the last two years, and we've been focusing on developing our portfolio and the projects we actually have.

Woche, was wirklich ziemlich schnell ist. Zudem haben wir vorgefertigte Badezimmer aus Italien verwendet. Sie wurden einfach eingebaut und das war's.
Um also Ihre Frage zu beantworten: Ja, es gibt viele Dinge, aus denen wir gelernt haben. Ich glaube, Vorfertigung bietet eine ganze Reihe interessanter Möglichkeiten.

PCS: Wenn wir an skandinavische Architektur denken, denken wir häufig an vorgefertigte Holzmodule. Arbeiten Sie auch damit?
OE: Wir arbeiten an einem solchen Projekt. Abgesehen davon hatten wir bereits zu einem früheren Zeitpunkt die Idee, das Gasklockan-Projekt in Holzbauweise zu erstellen. Das war aber nicht möglich, da man aus Brandschutzgründen in Holz nicht so hoch bauen kann. Wir fanden keinen Weg, um das Holz feuerfest zu machen. Das war allerdings vor zwei Jahren, mittlerweile gibt es wahrscheinlich eine Lösung.

PCS: Gibt es irgendetwas an dem Projekt, das Sie aus heutiger Sicht anders machen würden?
OE: Also, es gibt da eine Sache, die mir nicht gefällt. Wenn man die Lobby betritt, sind da zwei für die Briefkästen bestimmte Möbelelemente, die gefallen mir nicht.

PCS: Die Hochhausbewegung in Europa unterscheidet sich naturgemäß von jener in Asien und den USA. Gibt es einen Trend zum Hochhaus in Stockholm? Oder ist das Projekt Norra Tornen einzigartig?
OE: Wir wollten mit Herzog & de Meuron einen Turm bauen. Aber dann weigerte sich die Stadt Stockholm, das Grundstück, ein ehemaliges Gasometergelände, zu dekontaminieren. Da wir uns mit der Stadt nicht einigen konnten, ist das Projekt nun leider hinfällig. Es wäre aber auch unser letzter Hochhausbeitrag in der Stadt gewesen. Ich glaube nicht, dass es noch viele Orte in Stockholm gibt, die sich für ein Hochhaus eignen.

PCS: Sie haben nicht nur mit Herzog & de Meuron am Gasklockan-Projekt gearbeitet, sondern auch gemeinsam mit BIG ein Low-Rise-Projekt entwickelt. Es scheint, als würden Sie internationale Stararchitekten bevorzugen. Was halten die lokalen Architekten davon?
OE: Wir arbeiten auch mit vielen jungen Architekten zusammen. Nur mit den mittleren und großen Architekturbüros haben wir noch keine Projekte durchgeführt. Wir haben zum Beispiel in Hammarby sjöstad ein Projekt entwickelt. Es handelt sich um ein sehr schönes Grundstück in unmittelbarer Wassernähe. Mein Problem mit dem Gebiet war, dass sich die meisten der umliegenden Projekte glichen, es gab keine Unterschiede, keine Variationen. Also erwarben wir dort ein großes Grundstück für fast 200 Wohnungen und lobten einen Wettbewerb aus unter jungen Architekten, die gerade ihren Abschluss gemacht hatten, anstatt die großen Stararchitekten oder mittelgroßen Büros einzuladen. Wir haben die Gebäude letztendlich 2015 fertiggestellt und etwas völlig Neues geschaffen. Die meisten der beteiligten Architekten danken mir noch heute dafür, dass ich ihnen diese Möglichkeit gegeben habe. Wir arbeiten wirklich gerne mit jungen, kreativen Köpfen zusammen.

PCS: Are you only working in Sweden?
OE: For the moment, yes.

PCS: On your homepage you wrote "What motivates me is to help improve the city landscape in whatever way I can." What does that mean?
OE: It means in my opinion that in the last 30, 40 years—with the risk of sounding pretentious—there wasn't a lot of great architecture in Stockholm. I think there have been a few buildings here and there that are great. But for the last couple of years, all developments have been done by the big construction companies. And they lack vision, their whole idea is to industrialize and make everything look the same. That way, you can make money and you don't have to push for a great product. If you want to do something that looks a little bit different, they think it is going to cause cost overruns, and they don't want to do it. Consequently, these big developers have been lacking vision. I think most of these new developments look the same. By coming in and doing something new and different, you push other developers to become better as well. There have been a lot of new developments where the product is actually better, because people realize that if you create a good product, people are willing to pay more money. I really think that we have pushed others to do better. Of course, we are in this game to make money, but it's great to be able to make money doing something that you love and also contribute to the city.

PCS: Do you live in one of your own projects?
OE: No. Part of me would have wanted to live in each project, because I love each project so much, but I am happy where I live, I don't have to move.

PCS: Wie würden Sie sich selbst im Vergleich zu den anderen Bauträgern in der Stadt beschreiben?
OE: Ich denke, wir waren immer ein aufstrebendes Unternehmen, weil die anderen Bauträger uns nicht mochten. Weil wir etwas Neues machen. In Schweden herrschte Wohnungsnot. Wir haben daher eine neue Nische besetzt: Wir kauften Gewerbebauten und wandelten sie in Wohngebäude um. Parallel dazu haben wir neue Projekte entwickelt. Von 2012 bis 2017 stieg unser Bauvolumen von 112 Wohnungen auf 1500 Wohnungen pro Jahr an, das ist beachtlich. Das war aber nur möglich, weil die Nachfrage vorhanden war. Es war eine goldene Ära für viele Bauträger: Die Preise stiegen kontinuierlich. Viele neue Bauträger schossen aus dem Boden und bewarben sich um Grundstücke. Infolgedessen stiegen zum einen die Grundstücks- preise, und zum anderen wurde es zunehmend schwieriger, einen Kredit für den Kauf von Wohnungen zu bekommen. Dadurch sind wiederum die Nachfrage und unser Geschäft in den letzten zwei Jahren rückläufig. Wir haben uns auf die Entwicklung unseres Portfolios und der laufenden Projekte konzentriert.

PCS: Arbeiten Sie nur in Schweden?
OE: Aktuell ja.

PCS: Auf Ihrer Website schreiben Sie: „Meine Motivation ist es, zur Verbesserung der Stadtlandschaft beizu- tragen, wo immer ich kann." Was meinen Sie damit?
OE: Das bedeutet Folgendes: Auf die Gefahr hin, überheblich zu klingen, gab es meiner Meinung nach in den letzten 30, 40 Jahren kaum großartige Architektur in Stockholm. Hier und da entstanden, wie ich finde, ein paar herausragende Gebäude. In den letzten Jahren wurden sämtliche Projekte von großen Bauträgern entwickelt. Und denen fehlt es an Visionen; ihr Konzept besteht darin, zu rationalisieren und alles gleich aus- sehen zu lassen. Auf diese Weise kann man Geld verdienen und man kommt nicht in die Verlegenheit, sich um ein großartiges Resultat bemühen zu müssen. Bei allem, was ein bisschen anders aussieht, rechnen sie mit Kostenüberschreitung, und das ist nicht gewollt. Deshalb haben diese großen Projektentwickler keine Visionen. In meinen Augen sehen die meisten Neubau- projekte alle gleich aus. Wenn man aber etwas Neues, Anderes ausprobiert, ermutigt man andere Bauträger, sich ebenfalls weiterzuentwickeln. Bei vielen neuen Bauprojekten ist das Ergebnis tatsächlich besser, weil die Verantwortlichen erkannt haben, dass die Leute bereit sind, für ein gutes Produkt mehr Geld zu bezahlen. Ich glaube wirklich, dass wir andere dazu gebracht haben, sich zu verbessern. Natürlich wollen wir wie alle anderen auch, Geld verdienen, aber es ist großartig, mit etwas Geld zu verdienen, das man liebt und das auch der Stadt zugutekommt.

PCS: Wohnen Sie in einem Ihrer Projekte?
OE: Nein. Ein Teil von mir hätte in jedem meiner Projekte wohnen wollen, denn ich liebe sie alle sehr. Aber ich bin glücklich dort, wo ich bin, ich muss nicht umziehen.

Peter Cachola Schmal (Director Deutsches
**Architekturmuseum) in conversation with the
developer Oscar Engelbert in the office of Oscar
Properties**
Peter Cachola Schmal (Direktor Deutsches
Architekturmuseum) im Gespräch mit dem Bauherrn
Oscar Engelbert im Büro von Oscar Properties

View to the North from the city center
Blick vom Stadtzentrum Richtung Norden

Kjell Fallqvist in Conversation with Deutsches Architekturmuseum, Frankfurt am Main

Kjell Fallqvist, 65 years old and resident at Norra Tornen – Innovationen since 2019. He was chairman of the owners' community from 2019 to 2020.

DAM: Where did you live before and what were your reasons for moving into a high-rise?
Kjell Fallqvist: Our family lived on the 4th floor in an apartment with six rooms at Vanadisplan, which is close to the towers. My wife had always wanted to live in an apartment with a terrace and a good view, so when the towers were being built, we were very interested.

DAM: Were the architects behind the design important for your decision?
KF: Of course, aesthetics was very important, as was natural light. The very large windows in each apartment made Norra Tornen very desirable. Having lived in an older-style, traditional apartment, we really wanted to change to a modern style.

DAM: Would you move into a high-rise building again or are you missing anything, for example a garden?
KF: We moved into the Tower with the intention of staying here. We didn't have a garden in our previous homes, but now we have four terraces where it is possible to have some plants.

DAM: Sweden is not really known for high-rises. So, what is the reputation of residential towers in Stockholm?
KF: There are different views, and many people would like the city skyline to be kept low. But the general opinion is that as long as the high-rises are situated in the right location within the city, they are acceptable. Regulations are in place in this regard in order to preserve the traditional architecture of the city.

DAM: What are the benefits of living in a high-rise like Norra Tornen compared to ordinary Swedish homes, and what do you like most?
KF: The view is exceptional. I have 15 different water views from Lake Mälaren to the Baltic Sea, and I can see all the homes I've been living in during my 65 years.
There are 182 families living in the Tower, all using the same three lifts. So we meet friendly people on their way into and out of the building. It's always good to be able to get to know people and have a chat. Furthermore, the tower has a guest apartment, a dining room, a cinema, and a gym, which are available to use, to invite friends and meet other neighbors. Therefore, the Tower is very good from a social point of view.

Kjell Fallqvist im Gespräch mit Deutsches Architekturmuseum, Frankfurt am Main

Kjell Fallqvist (65 Jahre), seit 2019 Bewohner des Norra Tornen – Innovationen. Von 2019 bis 2020 war er Vorsitzender der Eigentümergemeinschaft.

DAM: Wo haben Sie vorher gelebt und was waren Ihre Gründe für den Umzug in ein Hochhaus?
Kjell Fallqvist: Unsere Familie wohnte in einer Sechs-Zimmer-Wohnung im vierten Stock am Vanadisplan, der in der Nähe der Norra Tornen liegt. Meine Frau wünschte sich schon immer eine Wohnung mit Terrasse und guter Aussicht, weshalb der Bau der Hochhäuser bei uns großes Interesse weckte.

DAM: Spielten die Architekten hinter dem Entwurf bei Ihrer Entscheidung eine Rolle?
KF: Natürlich war uns die Ästhetik sehr wichtig, ebenso natürliches Licht. Die großen Fenster in allen Wohnungen machten Norra Tornen sehr attraktiv. Wir lebten vorher in einer älteren, traditionellen Wohnung und wollten nun bewusst zu einem modernen Stil wechseln.

DAM: Würden Sie wieder in ein Hochhaus ziehen oder fehlt Ihnen etwas, beispielsweise ein Garten?
KF: Wir sind in das Hochhaus mit der Absicht eingezogen, hier zu bleiben. Unsere früheren Wohnungen hatten keinen Garten, jetzt haben wir vier Terrassen, die wir bepflanzen können.

DAM: Hochhäuser sind in Schweden nicht gerade üblich. Wie werden diese Wohntürme in Stockholm angenommen?
KF: Dazu gibt es verschiedene Ansichten. Viele möchten die Skyline der Stadt niedrig halten, aber insgesamt werden Hochhäuser akzeptiert, solange sie sich an der richtigen Stelle in der Stadt befinden. Es gibt hierzu Vorschriften, damit die traditionelle Architektur der Stadt erhalten bleibt.

DAM: Was sind die Vorteile eines Hochhauses wie Norra Tornen im Vergleich zu gewöhnlichen schwedischen Häusern und was gefällt Ihnen am besten an dieser Art des Wohnens?
KF: Die Aussicht ist außergewöhnlich. Mir eröffnet sich der Blick auf 15 verschiedene Gewässer, vom Mälaren-See bis zur Ostsee; und ich kann alle Orte sehen, an denen ich in den letzten 65 Jahren gelebt habe.
Im Norra Tornen – Innovationen leben 182 Familien und alle nutzen dieselben drei Aufzüge. Auf diese Weise begegnen wir auf unserem Weg in und aus dem Gebäude freundlichen Menschen. Es ist immer gut, die Möglichkeit zu haben, Leute kennenzulernen und sich zu unterhalten. Darüber hinaus verfügt der Turm über ein Gästeapartment, ein gemeinschaftlich nutzbares Esszimmer, ein Kino und einen Fitnessraum. Man kann Freunde dorthin einladen und Nachbarn treffen. Im Hinblick auf soziale Kontakte ist das Hochhaus also sehr vorbildlich.

Up to four balconies per apartment offer protected outdoor space above the roofs of the city.
Bis zu vier Balkone pro Wohnung bieten geschützten Außenraum über den Dächern der Stadt.

The rooms with the fixed glazed panoramic windows can be ventilated via ventilation flaps in the façade.
Über Lüftungsklappen in der Fassade können die Räume mit den fest verglasten Panoramafenstern belüftet werden.

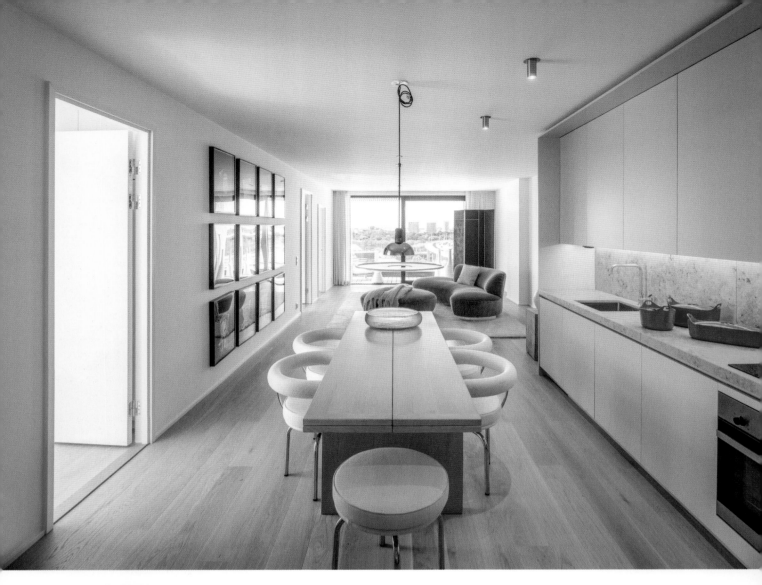

Living and dining area
Wohn- und Essbereich

DAM: Do the two buildings imply a big change for the Vasastaden district?
KF: Yes, the whole area has been transformed from the state at the end of the 1990's, when it was still a relatively industrial area, to one that is mainly residential and offers restaurants and shopping areas.

DAM: You were the chairman of the owners' community. Could you tell us something about the ownership structure of Norra Tornen – Innovationen?
KF: The owners are mostly young people in their thirties and fourties in the middle of their working career.

DAM: Are most of the apartments occupied by their owners or are they rented out or even empty because they were bought as an investment? What are the prices like compared to standard apartments in Stockholm?
KF: The rules in Sweden forbid buying apartments as an investment. You have to have a reason to rent out a property, such as a move for work or educational reasons, and the intention to return. This is why most of the apartments are owner-occupied.
The prices for an apartment of similar size and location compare to the tower apartments up to the 10th floor, then as you go up, the prices go up, and the penthouse is more than double the price.

DAM: What is your favorite place in the Innovationen Tower and why?
KF: In our apartment we really love the open-plan kitchen/living and dining area, where we can entertain our friends and prepare meals and drinks. And the very large windows that extend from floor to ceiling in every room fascinate me—they allow interesting perspectives of the outside and the city below.

DAM: Haben die beiden Norra-Tornen-Türme – Innovationen und Helix – eine große Veränderung für den Stadtteil Vasastaden mit sich gebracht?
KF: Ja, das gesamte Gebiet hat sich seit Ende der 1990er Jahre, als es noch ein recht industriell geprägtes Areal war, stark gewandelt. Heute ist es in erster Linie ein Wohngebiet mit Restaurants und Einkaufsmöglichkeiten.

DAM: Sie waren Vorsitzender der Eigentümergemeinschaft. Können Sie uns etwas über die Eigentümerstruktur von Norra Tornen – Innovationen erzählen?
KF: Bei den Eigentümerinnen und Eigentümer handelt es sich vorrangig um junge Leute im Alter zwischen 30 und 50 Jahren, die sich in der Mitte ihrer beruflichen Laufbahn befinden.

DAM: Werden die Wohnungen hauptsächlich von den Eigentümern bewohnt oder sind sie vermietet beziehungsweise stehen sogar leer, weil sie als Kapitalanlage erworben wurden? Wie verhalten sich die Kaufpreise im Vergleich zu Stockholmer Standardwohnungen?
KF: In Schweden ist es verboten, eine Wohnung als reines Investitionsobjekt zu kaufen. Man muss einen Grund vorweisen, um eine Wohnung zu vermieten – etwa einen Umzug aufgrund von Arbeitsplatzwechsel oder Ausbildung –, und man muss die Absicht haben, zurückzukehren. Daher bewohnen die meisten Eigentümer ihre Wohnung selbst.
Bis zum zehnten Stock sind die Quadratmeterpreise vergleichbar mit anderen Wohnungen ähnlicher Größe und Lage. Mit zunehmender Höhe ziehen die Preise allerdings an, das Penthouse ist dann mehr als doppelt so teuer.

DAM: Welcher ist Ihr Lieblingsort im Norra Tornen – Innovationen und warum?
KF: In unserer Wohnung lieben wir den Wohn- und Essbereich mit offener Küche. Hier können wir uns mit unseren Freunden unterhalten, während wir kochen oder schon anstoßen. Und mich faszinieren die sehr großen Fenster, die in allen Räumen vom Boden bis zur Decke reichen – sie ermöglichen interessante Perspektiven nach draußen und auf die Stadt unter uns.

Resident Kjell Fallqvist raves about living in the high-rise.
Bewohner Kjell Fallqvist schwärmt vom Wohnen im Hochhaus.

More Equal than Equal in the New Stockholm Plattenbau
James Taylor-Foster

Hemnet is the largest online property marketplace in Sweden. It's where many go to browse when they are looking to buy a house. With the thousands of brokers and hundreds of thousands of homes changing hands through this portal, I often browse the site—but not to scout out a home to buy. Rather, I'm fascinated by how homes for sale in Sweden are presented: spaces washed in shades of beige, warm grays, or soft pastel hues, books on shelves, wool blankets adorning inner-city balconies, flourishing plants, unlit candles, high-end soaps at washbasins, hardwood surfaces in kitchens adorned with *bulle* (sweet pastries) good enough to smell through the screen, a *kakelugn* or two (a typical Swedish ceramic fireplace), a smattering of IKEA peppered with Scandinavian design objects. More than any other, this marketplace has helped to transform the Swedish housing market into a self-fulfilling prophecy of sorts: in order to sell a place, that place must exude a character that satisfies a variety of aesthetic conditions. In turn, those buying a home demand that home to have a certain aesthetic. A property that is too shabby (not shabby-chic) or too bespoke may not sell as quickly nor as easily as one that fits the unspoken *Hemnet* mold: socially standardized, homogeneous and oh, so boring.

For some time now I have mused on what could account for this representational rule. Are the *lagom* images of apartment interiors that flood the marketing of the marketplace more of a tool to allow you, a prospective homeowner, to project your own life onto the space? Or is this in fact how many in Stockholm, the largest city in Sweden, actually decorate their environments? A photograph for *Hemnet* necessitates some staging, of course. The clutter of daily life is expelled, and traces of occupation are neutralized. And yet, more often than not, the bare bones of a home remain, be it the colors of the walls or the finish of the worktops. Having visited more homes in the Swedish capital than I can now recall, I'd argue for the latter. The tone and character of houses on *Hemnet* are not too distant from what homeowners strive to spend their days in.

To date I have not been invited to a home in Norra Tornen—two residential towers that slice the skyline of northern Stockholm. They stand together, slightly apart, bisected by a road—Torsgatan—in a developing district of the city called Hagastaden, located at the edge of Vasastan's older grain and building stock. (For the time being, this area is predominantly occupied by Karolinska, the city's largest university hospital.) Replace Torsgatan with a waterway and you have something akin to a hyper-formalist Colossus of Rhodes marking the boundary of the city. From my kitchen window on Södermalm, a large island due south, these towers soar, commanding the view entirely. In a city that is remarkably low-rise, with no other building neither as high nor as dominant as Innovationen and Helix, the names of the first and second tower respectively, they are hard to miss.

Gleicher als gleich im neuen Stockholmer Plattenbau
James Taylor-Foster

Hemnet ist Schwedens größter Online-Immobilienmarktplatz. Hier suchen viele, die ein Haus kaufen wollen. Ich stöbere oft in diesem Portal, auf dem Tausende Makler vertreten sind und Hunderttausende Immobilien den Besitzer wechseln – allerdings nicht, um ein Haus zu kaufen. Mich fasziniert vielmehr, wie die zum Verkauf stehenden Häuser in Schweden präsentiert werden: Man findet Räume, die in Beige-, warmen Grau- oder zarten Pastelltönen gehalten sind, auf gut bestückte Bücherregale, Wolldecken auf innerstädtischen Balkonen, blühende Pflanzen, dekorative Kerzen, hochwertige Seifen am Waschbeckenrand, Küchentheken aus Hartholz, auf denen *bulle* (süße Gebäckteilchen) thronen und gleichsam aus dem Bildschirm duften, ferner ein oder gar zwei *kakelugn* (ein typisch schwedischer Kachelofen), hier und da ein IKEA-Element, veredelt mit skandinavischen Designobjekten. Dieser Marktplatz hat wie kein anderer dazu beigetragen, den schwedischen Wohnungsmarkt in eine Art sich bewahrheitende Prophezeiung zu verwandeln: Um verkäuflich zu sein, muss die Immobilie eine Vielzahl von ästhetischen Voraussetzungen erfüllen und eine ganz bestimmte Ausstrahlung haben. Umgekehrt erwarten die potenziellen Käufer genau diese Ästhetik. Ein Objekt, das zu schäbig (nicht zu verwechseln mit *shabby-chic*) oder zu individuell erscheint, verkauft sich möglicherweise nicht so schnell und leicht wie eines, das dem inoffiziell geltenden *Hemnet*-Schema entspricht: sozial standardisiert, einheitlich und, ach, so langweilig.

Seit einiger Zeit denke ich darüber nach, was es mit dieser Art der Präsentation auf sich hat, die die Marketingkanäle des Immobilienmarktplatzes überschwemmt. Sind diese *Lagom*-Bilder von ausgewogenen Wohnungsinterieurs (*lagom* bedeutet auf Schwedisch so viel wie „gerade richtig", „in Balance") ein Mittel zum Zweck, damit angehende Hausbesitzer ihr eigenes Leben in diese Räume projizieren können? Oder gestalten tatsächlich viele Menschen in Stockholm, der größten Stadt Schwedens, ihren Wohnumfeld in diesem Stil? Ein Foto für die Plattform *Hemnet* bedarf natürlich einer gewissen Inszenierung. Die Unordnung des Alltags wird ausgeblendet, Nutzungsspuren werden neutralisiert. Und so verbleibt meist nur das bloße Gerippe einer Wohnung, die Farbe der Wände oder die Ausführung der Oberflächen. Ich kenne unzählige Häuser und Wohnungen in der schwedischen Hauptstadt aus eigener Anschauung – und auf Basis dieser Erfahrung würde ich meinen, dass sich die Schweden tatsächlich gerne so einrichten. Der Charakter der Häuser auf *Hemnet* und die Atmosphäre, die sie ausstrahlen, weichen kaum ab von dem Ambiente, das Eigentümer anstreben.

Eingeladen wurde ich bis heute noch in keine der Wohnung in Norra Tornen – das Ensemble besteht aus zwei Wohntürmen, die die Skyline des Stockholmer Nordens zerschneiden. Sie stehen nebeneinander, nur getrennt durch eine Straße, die Torsgatan, im neu entstehenden Stadtteil Hagastaden und am Rande des älteren Gebäudebestands des Stadtteils Vasastan. (Zurzeit ist dieses Gebiet vor allem geprägt von der Karolinska, dem größten Universitätskrankenhaus der Stadt.) Ersetzt man die Torsgatan gedanklich durch eine

Apartments at Norra Tornen – as made for Hemnet, Sweden's largest online marketplace for real estate
Wohnungen in Norra Tornen – wie gemacht für Hemnet, Schwedens größten Onlinemarktplatz für Immobilien

To date, there is not any other residential project in Stockholm able to compete with Norra Tornen's scale, overt *lagom* luxury, and contemporary international architectural pedigree. Given this, a long and divisive planning process underpins its birth. The site was first tabled in 2008. Two towers, conceived to be perceived and commissioned as one entity, were proposed under the provisional name *Tors torn*: the Tower of Thor. The site was demarcated—a height and a silhouette outlined—by Aleksander Wolodarski, the former city architect. The scale and location of the proposed high-rises led to considerable debate, during which Wolodarski and *Skönhetsrådet*, the so-called 'Beauty Council', an advisory body charged with inspecting city planning and construction proposals, locked heads. The competition through which OMA was commissioned had not yet taken place, but the Beauty Council's core concern centered on the sheer size of the proposed towers. The city architect was criticized for suggesting something too grand, too monumental for Stockholm's gentle skyline of green and black roofs and slender spires.[1] Following years of discussion, a building permit was approved, albeit controversially, in 2015—and then bitterly and unsuccessfully contested by local residents and Sweden's Civil Aviation Authority.

After the first developer tasked with the project withdrew, Oscar Properties entered the fray. This company, founded in 2004 and managed by Oscar Engelbert, has steered it to completion. As one of the very few Swedish property developers committed to commissioning nationally and internationally acclaimed architecture studios, their business concept, in their own words, is to build "the most attractive homes on the market with art, design and architecture as the foundation stones."[2] By this metric, they have lived up to their aspiration: with a completed wood-clad residential project by the Danish starchitecture practice Bjarke Ingels Group (BIG), and a project now in a state of limbo designed by the Swiss starchitecture partnership Herzog & De Meuron, Norra Tornen represents the first major project in Sweden designed by OMA— one of the most acclaimed architectural practices of our time. This is something that should not go unnoticed; in the often protectionist commissioning environment that architectural practices tend to be confronted with in Sweden, this is a considerable achievement. At the outset, the project promised a lot: "the informal appearance of the towers will express domesticity," a press release published by OMA asserted in 2013—"perhaps even humanism."[3] A publicly accessible bar and exhibition space was slated for the upper floors of one tower. A public library, alongside a children's center and retail spaces, were proposed for the ground floors. Seven years on, little of these have materialized.

Nevertheless, amid a housing market in which high-level balance (*lagom*) is highly desirable to one portion of prospective buyers, Norra Tornen is an interesting case. It marks a simultaneous continuation of and deviation from a fundamental rule of thumb that has been driving Swedish housing projects for decades. The apartments are deluxe and have a price tag to match. The search for

Large terraces form where the structure jumps back.
Dort wo der Baukörper zurückspringt, bilden sich großflächige Terrassen aus.

Wasserstraße, so avanciert das Ensemble zu einer Art hyperformalistischem Koloss von Rhodos, der die Stadtgrenze markiert. Die in die Höhe strebenden Türme beherrschen die Aussicht aus meinem Küchenfenster auf Södermalm, einer großen Insel im Süden. In einer Stadt mit bemerkenswert niedriger Traufhöhe, in der kein anderes Gebäude derart hoch oder dominant ist wie Innovationen und Helix – so heißen die beiden Türme –, sind diese kaum zu übersehen.

Bis heute kann es kein anderes Wohnprojekt in Stockholm mit dem Maßstab, dem offenkundigen *Lagom*-Luxus und der Internationalität der zeitge-nössischen Architekten von Norra Tornen aufnehmen. Entsprechend lang und kontrovers war der Planungs-prozess, der dem Projekt vorausging. Der Standort kam erstmals 2008 auf den Tisch. Unter dem provisorischen Namen „Tors torn" – der Turm von Thor – waren zwei Türme vorgesehen, die als Einheit wahrgenommen und ausgeschrieben werden sollten. Der ehemalige Stadtarchitekt Aleksander Wolodarski grenzte das Grundstück ab und umriss die Höhe und Silhouette. Die Größe und der Standort der geplanten Hochhäuser hatten erhebliche Debatten zur Folge, im Zuge derer sich Wolodarski und der *Skönhetsrådet* – der sogenannte „Schönheitsbeirat", ein Gestaltungsbeirat, beauftragt mit der Prüfung von Stadtplanungs- und Bauvorhaben – in die Haare gerieten. Der Wettbewerb, den OMA später für sich entscheiden sollte, war noch nicht ausgeschrieben, aber das wesentliche Bedenken des Gestaltungsbeirats betraf die enorme Größe der Türme. Der Stadtarchitekt wurde kritisiert, weil er etwas vorgeschlagen hatte, das zu gewaltig, zu monumental für Stockholms sanfte, von grünen und schwarzen Dächern sowie schlanken Türmen geprägte Skyline war.[1] Nach jahrelangen Diskussionen wurde 2015 eine, wenn auch umstrittene, Baugenehmigung erteilt – und dann von Anwohnern und der schwedischen Zivilluft-fahrtbehörde erbittert, aber erfolglos angefochten.

Nachdem sich der erste mit dem Projekt betraute Entwickler zurückgezogen hatte, trat Oscar Properties auf den Plan. Das 2004 von Oscar Engelbert gegründete und geführte Unternehmen – einer der wenigen schwedischen Bauträger, die national und international anerkannte Architekturbüros beauftragen – hat das Projekt zum Abschluss gebracht. Das Geschäftskonzept von Oscar Properties besteht nach eigenen Worten darin, „die attraktivsten Häuser auf dem Markt" zu bauen, und zwar „mit Kunst, Design und Architektur als Grundsteinen".[2] In diesem Sinne ist das Unternehmen seinem Anspruch gerecht geworden: Neben dem bereits fertiggestellten, holzverkleideten Wohnprojekt des dänischen Stararchitekturbüros Bjarke Ingels Group (BIG) und einem noch in der Schwebe befindlichen Projekt der Schweizer Stararchitekten Herzog & de Meuron, ist Norra Tornen das erste Projekt von OMA, einem der renommiertesten Architekturbüros unserer Zeit, in Schweden. Das ist eine beachtliche Errungenschaft angesichts der oftmals protektionis-tischen Beauftragungssituation, mit der Architekturbüros in Schweden konfrontiert sind. Zu Beginn des Projekts wurde viel versprochen: „Das informelle Erscheinungs-bild der Türme wird Häuslichkeit ausdrücken", so eine Pressemitteilung von OMA im Jahr 2013, „vielleicht sogar Humanismus".[3] In den oberen Stockwerken des einen Turms waren eine öffentlich Bar und ein Aus-stellungsraum vorgesehen. Im Erdgeschoss sollten eine

"Torsplan 10" on *Hemnet*, the address now ascribed to the project, lists a number of the altogether three hundred apartments that make up the towers that are for sale. One particular apartment, located on the twenty-third floor of Helix and teetering sixty-five meters above the street level, comprises eighty-eight square meters with two bedrooms and three independent terraces. (The smallest residence in the towers is forty-four square meters, while the penthouse is two hundred and seventy-one square meters.) The building's housing association, the property description notes, will offer, when completed, amenities including a guest apartment, a private cinema, a gym, and a garage. The list price for this apartment is 10 895 000 Swedish kronor, a little over one million euro, and constitutes an expensive apartment even by Stockholm's standards—a symptom and a result of fledgling interest in the city from investors both near and far. It was reported that one of the larger apartments, a two hundred square meter unit, had sold for forty-two million kronor, cementing the highrise as among the most valuable real estate in the city.[4]

The local response has been mixed, and charged. Some see the towers as optimistic symbols of the gradually increasing vitality of the city—that in a new phase of high-rise densification, long overdue, Stockholm can finally take its place among other capitals that it ranks alongside. Others see the towers as an embodiment of the sweeping changes that the Swedish state has borne witness to in recent years. Until now, luxury apartments had been heard of but never seen. The debate that surrounded the project long before it broke ground continued when construction began. In 2018, *Arkitekturupproret* (The Architecture Uprising), a controversial Swedish group committed to banning contemporary architecture from the city (read: any architectural project that has not been designed to appear classical, medieval, or to be an example of Swedish grace, and so on) nominated Norra Tornen for the so-called *Kaspar Kalkon* (Kaspar Turkey) prize.[5] In the same way that the infamous Carbuncle Cup mocks architectural awards in the United Kingdom, this award, which mocks the Kasper Salin prize—an annual award given by a jury to a building in Sweden that exhibits high architectural quality—, sought to label the towers as the year's ugliest.

Reinier de Graaf, the architect in charge of the project, has been keen to reaffirm that the practice inherited the building envelopes first sculpted by Wolodarski. This envelope demanded a staggered form, and the architects' response is, in many ways, a clever response to a somewhat limiting brief. To this end, it has architectural ties. It has a certain relation to the escaping capsules of Kisho Kurokawa's Nakagin Tower in Tokyo, one of the most brutally charming residential buildings in one the densest urban environments in the world. It recalls the cubic assemblage of Moshe Safdie's Habitat 67 in Montréal, quadrupling its height. It could appear to be a contemporary cousin of the residential towers of the Barbican in London, a seminal Modernist structure designed by Chamberlin, Powell and Bon in the 1950s. And yet its differences to these projects are stark, and can only be observed

öffentliche Bibliothek, eine Einrichtung für Kinder sowie Einzelhandelsflächen untergebracht werden. Sieben Jahre später ist wenig davon Realität geworden.

Nichtsdestotrotz ist Norra Tornen im Kontext eines Wohnungsmarktes, in dem ein Teil der Käufer größtmögliche Ausgewogenheit (lagom) verlangt, ein interessanter Fall. Das Projekt führt die Faustregel *lagom*, die die schwedische Wohnbauprojekte seit Jahrzehnten prägt, fort und weicht zugleich von ihr ab. Die Wohnungen sind luxuriös und kosten entsprechend. Sucht man auf *Hemnet* nach „Torsplan 10", der nun offiziellen Adresse des Projekts, so erhält man eine Aufstellung einiger der insgesamt dreihundert Wohnungen, aus denen sich die Türme zusammensetzen, die zum Verkauf stehen. Eine davon befindet sich im 23. Stock des Helix, 65 Meter über dem Straßenniveau. Sie hat 88 Quadratmeter, zwei Schlafzimmer und drei Terrassen. (Die kleinste Wohnung in den Türmen ist 44 Quadratmeter groß, während das Penthouse über 271 Quadratmeter verfügt.) Laut Objektbeschreibung wird die Wohnungsbaugesellschaft nach Fertigstellung des Norra Tornen – Helix Ausstattungsmerkmale wie eine Gästewohnung, ein privates Kino, ein Fitnessstudio und eine Garage anbieten. Der Listenpreis für die Wohnung im 23. Stock beträgt 10 895 000 Schwedische Kronen, also etwas mehr als eine Million Euro. Das ist selbst für Stockholmer Verhältnisse teuer – und sowohl Symptom als auch Ergebnis des wachsenden Interesses von Investoren an der Stadt. Wie zu lesen war, wurde eine der größeren Wohnungen (im Bereich von 200 Quadratmetern) für 42 Millionen Kronen verkauft, was Norra Tornen zu einer der wertvollsten Immobilien der Stadt macht.[4]

Die Reaktionen vor Ort waren gemischt und emotionsgeladen. Einige betrachten die Türme als hoffnungsvolle Symbole einer immer lebendiger werdenden Stadt – als Zeichen dafür, dass Stockholm in einer neuen, längst überfälligen Phase der Verdichtung mittels Hochhäuser endlich seinen Platz neben gleichwertigen Hauptstädten einnimmt. Andere sehen in den Türmen eine Manifestation der tief greifenden Veränderungen, die der schwedische Staat in den letzten Jahren erfahren hat. Bislang hatte man von Luxuswohnungen gehört, aber nie welche gesehen. Die Debatte, die das Projekt lange vor dem ersten Spatenstich begleitete, setzte sich nach Baubeginn fort. *Arkitekturupproret* (Architekturaufstand) – eine umstrittene schwedische Gruppe, deren Ziel es ist, zeitgenössische Architektur (sprich: jedes Architekturprojekt, das nicht klassisch, mittelalterlich oder beispielhaft schwedisch anmutet) aus der Stadt fernzuhalten – nominierte Norra Tornen 2018 für den sogenannten „Kaspar Kalkon"-Preis (*kalkon* ist das schwedische Wort für Truthahn).[5] So wie der berüchtigte Carbuncle Cup Architekturpreise im Vereinigten Königreich ins Lächerliche zieht, zeichnete dieser Preis – in Anspielung auf den Kasper-Salin-Preis, der jährlich einem schwedischen Gebäude von hoher architektonischer Qualität verliehen wird – die Türme als hässlichstes Bauwerk des Jahres aus.

Reinier de Graaf, der verantwortliche Projektarchitekt, legte Wert darauf zu betonen, dass OMA das Konzept der ursprünglich von Wolodarski entworfenen Gebäudehüllen übernehmen musste. Diese verlangte nach einer gestaffelten Form – und die Antwort der Architekten ist in vielerlei Hinsicht eine kluge Reaktion auf die eher

Chamberlin, Powell and Bon, Barbican Estate, 1965–76

Moshe Safdie, Habitat 67, Montreal, 1966–67

from up close. What appears from a distance to be a warm, brown façade, adhering to Stockholm's prescribed color palette, is highly sophisticated in its materiality. Ribbed pigmented concrete, brushed with exposed multi-colored aggregate pebble, gives the towers a benign radiance that, at certain moments in the day, softens their scale.

It is a boon for Stockholm to have a building executed by a practice so influential, and especially so given the fact that this phenomenon is tragically rare. It is, nonetheless, a "plattenbau for the rich". De Graaf's words highlight much: on the one hand, it is a prefabricated concrete structure that through the finesse of its outward material expression subverts the stereotypes of housing dating from the *Million Programme* era, which weigh heavy in the minds of many. On the other hand, it stands for the precise opposite: a place that very few Stockholmers will ever be able to afford.

Norra Tornen stands out because it stands alone. It is, for many, a face of a possible future that they would prefer not to see. Stockholm, for a complex myriad of reasons and opinions, has so far resisted high-rise densification in the city center. It may in fact prove to be one of those rare architectural projects that sits outside of its own time—not due to its architecture *per se* but due to the city that it overlooks in solitude.

[1] https://www.svd.se/arkitekt-far-hard-kritik (letzter Zugriff: 09.08.2020)
[2] https://oscarproperties.com/en/about-us/ foundation-values/ (letzter Zugriff: 09.08.2020)
[3] https://oma.eu/news/oma-and-oscar-properties-win-tors-torn-competition-in-stockholm (letzter Zugriff: 09.08.2020)
[4] https://www.svd.se/lyxlagenhet-i-torn-sald--for-42-miljoner (letzter Zugriff: 09.08.2020)
[5] http://www.arkitekturupproret.se/2018/12/01/kasper-kalkon-priset-2018-vilken-ar-arets-fulaste-nya-byggnad/norra-tornen-innovationen-i-hagastaden-stockholm-foto-helen-bark/ (letzter Zugriff: 09.08.2020)

limitierenden Vorgaben. In diesem Sinne zeigen sich architektonische Bezüge: Norra Tornen hat eine gewisse Ähnlichkeit mit Kisho Kurokawas Nakagin Tower in Tokio mit seinen auskragenden Kapseln – auf brutale Weise eines der charmantesten Wohngebäude in einer der dichtesten städtischen Umgebungen der Welt. Das Projekt erinnert an die kubische Assemblage von Moshe Safdies Habitat 67 in Montréal, allerdings viermal so hoch. Es erscheint wie ein zeitgenössischer Cousin der Wohntürme des Barbican Centre in London – ein bahnbrechendes modernistisches Bauwerk, das in den 1950er Jahren von Chamberlin, Powell und Bon entworfen wurde.
Und doch sind die Unterschiede zu diesen Projekten frappant, wenn auch nur aus unmittelbarer Nähe erkennbar. Was aus der Ferne wie eine warme, braune Fassade erscheint, die sich an die vorgeschriebene Farbpalette Stockholms hält, besticht durch eine höchst raffinierte Materialität: Der pigmentierte und gerippte Beton, angereichert mit sichtbaren, mehrfarbigen Kieselsteinen, verleiht den Türmen eine freundliche Ausstrahlung und relativiert dadurch ihre Größe zu gewissen Tageszeiten.

Ein Gebäude aus der Feder eines derart einflussreichen Büros ist ein Segen für Stockholm. Vor allem angesichts der Tatsache, dass dies leider nur selten vorkommt. Nichtsdestotrotz ist das Ensemble ein „Plattenbau für Reiche". Mit diesen Worten bringt De Graaf zwei Dinge zum Ausdruck: Einerseits handelt es sich um einen Plattenbau, der dank der Finesse seiner äußeren Beschaffenheit die Stereotypen des Wohnungsbaus aus der Zeit des *Million Programme* unterläuft, die in den Köpfen vieler Menschen schwer nachwirken. Auf der anderen Seite steht diese Architektur für das genaue Gegenteil: Sie ist ein Ort, den sich nur wenige Stockholmer jemals werden leisten können.

Norra Tornen sticht hervor, weil es einzigartig ist. Für viele ist das Projekt das Antlitz einer möglichen Zukunft, die sie lieber nicht erleben möchten. Stockholm hat sich der Hochhausverdichtung in der Innenstadt aus einer Vielzahl von Gründen bisher verwehrt. Norra Tornen könnte sich in der Tat als eines der seltenen Architekturprojekte erweisen, das aus der eigenen Zeit fällt – nicht aufgrund seiner Architektur *per se*, sondern im Hinblick auf die Stadt, die es einsam überblickt.

Biography

James Taylor-Foster is a writer, editor and curator working in the fields of architecture, design, e-culture, and technology. He is the curator of contemporary architecture and design at ArkDes, Sweden's national center for architecture and design, in Stockholm. Trained in architecture, he was formerly editor-at-large for *ArchDaily*. In 2016 he co-curated the Nordic Pavilion at the 15th Biennale Architettura di Venezia and in 2018 participated in the central exhibition at the 16th.

Biografie

James Taylor-Foster ist Autor, Herausgeber und Kurator und arbeitet in den Bereichen Architektur, Design, E-Culture und Technologie. Er ist Kurator für zeitgenössische Architektur und Gestaltung am schwedischen Zentrum für Architektur und Design ArkDes in Stockholm. Nach seinem Architekturstudium war er Redakteur bei *ArchDaily*. 2016 war er Co-Kurator des Nordischen Pavillons im Rahmen der 15. Biennale Architettura di Venezia und 2018 an der zentralen Ausstellung der 16. Architekturbiennale beteiligt.

The pigmented ribbed concrete, which is enriched with mer-colored pebbles, creates a warm and friendly appearance in the sunlight analogous to Stockholm's earthy color palette.
Der pigmentierte Rippenbeton, der mit mehrfarbigen Kieselsteinen angereichert ist, erzeugt im Sonnenlicht ein warmes und freundliches Erscheinungsbild analog zu Stockholms erdiger Farbpalette.

Left side: The public roof terrace of the Blique Hotel at Gävlegatan offers the best view of the towers.
Linke Seite: Von der öffentlichen Dachterrasse des Hotel Blique in der Gävlegatan hat man die beste Aussicht auf die beiden Türme.

Top right: Peter Körner and Stefanie Lampe (Curators and Coordination IHP 2020, together with Jonas Malzahn [not in this photo])
Oben rechts: Peter Körner und Stefanie Lampe (Kuratoren und Koordination IHP 2020, gemeinsam mit Jonas Malzahn [nicht im Bild])

Center: Peter Cachola Schmal (Director Deutsches Architekturmuseum) and developer Oscar Engelbert at the office of Oscar Properties
Mitte: Peter Cachola Schmal (Direktor Deutsches Architekturmuseum) und Bauherr Oscar Engelbert im Büro von Oscar Properties

Rogers Stirk Harbour & Partners, London, UK
Großbritannien
3 WORLD TRADE CENTER, New York, NY, USA

Diller Scofidio + Renfro, New York NY, USA
15 HUDSON YARDS, New York, NY, USA

CetraRuddy Architecture, New York NY, USA
ARO, New York, NY, USA

Foster + Partners, London, UK Großbritannien
COMCAST TECHNOLOGY CENTER, Philadelphia, PA, USA

Rafael Viñoly Architects, New York, NY, USA
NEMA CHICAGO, Chicago IL, USA

Studio Gang Architects, Chicago IL, USA
MIRA, San Francisco, CA, USA

Richard Meier & Partners Architects, New York NY, USA
TORRES CUARZO, Mexico City Mexiko-Stadt, **Mexico** Mexiko

LEGORRETA, Mexico City Mexiko-Stadt, **Mexico** Mexiko
MIYANA, TORRE CHAPULÍN, Mexico City Mexiko-Stadt, **Mexico** Mexiko

Estudio de Arquitectura Alonso Balaguer SLP, Barcelona, **Spain** Spanien
BACATÁ TOWER, Bogotá, Colombia Kolumbien

Magnus Kaminiarz & Cie. Architektur, Frankfurt am Main, Germany Deutschland
GRAND TOWER, Frankfurt am Main, Germany Deutschland

BIG – Bjarke Ingels Group, Copenhagen Kopenhagen/**New York, NY, Denmark** Dänemark/**USA**
OMNITURM, Frankfurt am Main, Germany Deutschland

Skidmore, Owings & Merrill LLP, Chicago, IL, USA
THE STRATFORD, London, UK Großbritannien

Dominique Perrault Architecture, Paris, France Frankreich
5th EXTENSION OF THE EUROPEAN COURT OF JUSTICE, Luxembourg Luxemburg

Ateliers Jean Nouvel, Paris, France Frankreich
LA MARSEILLAISE, Marseille, France Frankreich

Morphosis Architects, Culver City, CA, USA
CASABLANCA FINANCE CITY TOWER, Casablanca, Morocco Marokko

Foster + Partners, London, UK Großbritannien
NATIONAL BANK OF KUWAIT – NBK TOWER Kuwait City Kuwait-Stadt, **Kuwait**

Skidmore, Owings & Merrill LLP, Chicago, IL, USA
TIANJIN CTF FINANCE CENTER, Tianjin, China

Zaha Hadid Architects, London, UK Großbritannien
LEEZA SOHO, Beijing Peking, China

Safdie Architects, Somerville, MA, USA
GOLDEN DREAM BAY, Qinhuangdao, China

gmp Architekten von Gerkan, Marg und Partner,
Hamburg, Germany Deutschland
POLY GREENLAND PLAZA, Shanghai, China

GRAFT, Berlin, Germany Deutschland
LUXE LAKE TOWERS, Chengdu, China

Kohn Pedersen Fox Associates, New York, NY, USA
MGM COTAI, Macau, China

WOHA, Singapore Singapur
SKY GREEN, Taichung, Taiwan

Zaha Hadid Architects, London, UK Großbritannien
MORPHEUS HOTEL & RESORTS AT CITY OF
DREAMS, Macau, China

Atkins, London, UK Großbritannien
LANDMARK 81, Ho Chi Minh City Ho-Chi-Minh-
Stadt, Vietnam

BIG – Bjarke Ingels Group, Copenhagen
Kopenhagen/New York, NY, Denmark Dänemark/
USA
SHENZHEN ENERGY HEADQUARTERS, Shenzhen,
China

Heatherwick Studio, London, UK Großbritannien
EDEN, Singapore Singapur

Kohn Pedersen Fox Associates, New York, NY, USA
CHINA RESOURCES TOWER, Shenzhen, China

Kohn Pedersen Fox Associates, New York, NY, USA
ROBINSON TOWER, Singapore Singapur

CCDI Group, Shenzhen, China
SHENZHEN BAIDU HEADQUARTERS, Shenzhen,
China

Finalist 2020

BIG – Bjarke Ingels Group
OMNITURM
Frankfurt am Main, Germany Deutschland

Architects Architekten **BIG – Bjarke Ingels Group,
Copenhagen** Kopenhagen/**New York, NY, Denmark**
Dänemark/**USA**
Project architects Projektarchitekten **Bjarke Ingels,
Andreas Klok Pedersen, Lorenzo Boddi**
Architects of record Lokale Architekten **B&V Braun
Canton Park Architekten**
Client Bauherr **Commerzbank**
Structural engineers Tragwerksplanung
PfeiferINTERPLAN BAUBERATUNG
MEP Haustechnik **Techdesign; Elektroplanung K.
Dörflinger**

Height Höhe **190 m**
Stories Geschosse **45**
Site area Grundstücksfläche **1800 m²**

Building footprint Bebaute Fläche **1400 m²**
Gross floor area Bruttogeschossfläche **70 000 m²**
Structure Konstruktion **Reinforced concrete and steel**
Stahlbeton und Stahl
Completion Fertigstellung **December** Dezember **2019**
Main use Hauptnutzung **Mixed use comprising offices
and apartments** Mischnutzung aus Büros und Wohnen

Sustainability:
pursuing LEED Platinum certification; high-quality
envelope; dedicated outdoor air system with heat
recovery; low-temperature radiant heating and
cooling; high-efficiency chiller; high-efficiency LED
lighting; connection to the district heating system

Nachhaltigkeit:
LEED-Platin-Zertifizierung angestrebt; hochwertige Hülle;
spezielles Außenluftsystem mit Wärmerückgewinnung;
Niedertemperatur-Strahlungsheizung und -kühlung;
Hochleistungskühler; Hochleistungs-LED-Beleuchtung;
Anschluss an das Fernwärmenetz

Series of terraces
Serie von Terrassen

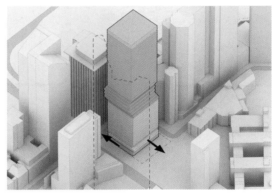

Shifted public spaces
Verschobene öffentliche Räume

**The classical
steel and glass cuboid
gets a hip-swing.**
Der klassische
Stahl-und-Glas-Quader
erhält einen Hüftschwung.

Lobby
Empfangshalle

Due to the hip-swing, balconies are created in the floors for residential use.
Durch den Hüftschwung entstehen in den Geschossen zur Wohnnutzung Balkone.

Omniturm with its office, residential, and public spaces is Germany's first mixed-use high-rise building. The tower is designed as a slender, rational stack of floors, with two sculptural movements following the changes in function.

The lower floors are shifted back and forth to create terraces and arcades for the public levels, thereby anchoring the building in its surroundings. In the middle of the tower, which accommodates the residential units, the floors slide outwards in a spiral movement following the course of the sun. The 'hip-swing' lends the tower lightness and dynamics and marks a turning point in Frankfurt's city center, which is characterized by office towers that are monotonous regarding their use. This change in the silhouette creates non-public outdoor spaces with impressive views for the residents. The upper section of the Omniturm returns to the simple, efficient addition of floors, and the metal-glass façade rises evenly. This results in flexible floor plans for office use.

Due to its location in the middle of the banking district, the Omniturm high-rise is surrounded by a variety of retail, catering, and cultural facilities. The tower is located at Europe's first intersection with high-rise buildings taller than 100 meters at all four corners.

The lower levels of the tower are open to the public and connected to the neighboring site. A new park for the city center is being created there on the former Deutsche Bank site. The public areas in the podium provide column-free spaces with particularly high ceilings for coworking areas, a cafeteria, and a function room. This was already agreed with the City of Frankfurt during the design phase. The tower is to be animated with active (business) life through a mixture of conventional office tower tenants and smaller start-ups.

The supporting structure of the tower with main and secondary beams made of precast reinforced concrete elements does not require corner supports. Only the floor slabs and the building core with the elevators and the supply shafts are made of in-situ concrete. As there are comparatively few additional structural details, the advantages of a precast concrete construction method came into effect. The shifting of the floors along the vertical axis was optimized so that inclinations could be minimized. Due to the tightly delimited inner-city location, it was necessary to implement the four basement levels in 'floating' top-down construction.

Der Omniturm mit seinen Büro-, Wohn- und öffentlichen Räumen ist Deutschlands erstes Hochhaus mit gemischter Nutzung. Der Turm ist als schlanke, rationale Stapelung von Geschossen gestaltet, mit zwei den Funktionswechseln folgenden skulpturalen Bewegungen.

Die unteren Stockwerke springen vor und zurück, um Terrassen und Arkaden für die öffentlich genutzten Ebenen zu ermöglichen, und verankern das Gebäude in seiner Umgebung. Im mittleren Teil des Turms, wo sich die Wohnetagen befinden, schieben sich die Geschosse in einer dem Lauf der Sonne folgenden Spiralbewegung nach außen. Der „Hüftschwung" verleiht dem Turm Leichtigkeit und Dynamik und markiert eine Wende in der von in ihrer Nutzung monotonen Bürotürmen geprägten Frankfurter Innenstadt. Durch diese Veränderung in der Silhouette entstehen nicht öffentliche Außenräume mit beeindruckenden Aussichten für die Bewohner. Der obere Teil des Omniturms kehrt zurück zur einfachen, effizienten Addition der Etagen, und die Metall-Glas-Fassade steigt gleichmäßig in die Höhe. So entstehen flexible Grundrisse für die Büronutzung.

Aufgrund seiner Lage inmitten des Bankenviertels ist der Omniturm von einer Vielzahl an Einzelhandels-, Gastronomie- und Kulturangeboten umgeben. Der Turm steht an Europas erster Straßenkreuzung, die an allen vier Ecken Hochhäuser mit mehr als 100 Metern Höhe aufweist.

Die unteren Geschosse des Turms sind öffentlich zugänglich und mit dem Nachbargrundstück verbunden. Dort entsteht auf dem ehemaligen Areal der Deutschen Bank ein neuer Park für die Innenstadt. Die öffentlichen Bereiche im Sockel bieten besonders hohe, stützenfreie Räume für Coworking-Flächen, eine Cafeteria und einen Veranstaltungsraum. Dies wurde schon während der Entwurfsphase mit der Stadt Frankfurt vereinbart. Das Hochhaus soll durch eine Mischung von traditionellen Bürohochhausmietern und kleineren Start-ups mit aktivem (Geschäfts-)Leben erfüllt werden.

Das Tragwerk des Turms mit Haupt- und Nebenträgern aus Stahlbetonfertigteilen kommt ohne Eckstützen aus. Nur die Geschossdecken sowie der Gebäudekern mit den Aufzügen und den Versorgungsschächten bestehen aus Ortbeton. Da es ansonsten verhältnismäßig wenig konstruktive Details gibt, kamen die Vorteile einer Betonfertigteilbauweise zum Tragen. Die Geschossverschiebung entlang der Vertikalachse wurde so optimiert, dass Schrägstellungen minimiert werden konnten. Aufgrund des eng umgrenzten innerstädtischen Standorts war es erforderlich, die vier Untergeschosse in „schwebender" Deckelbauweise auszuführen.

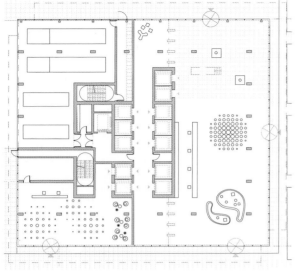

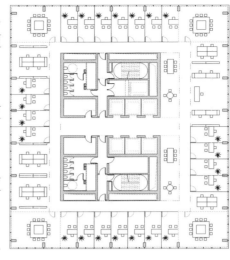

Floor plans Grundrisse
Ground floor plan (top left)
Typical office floor plan (top right)
Typical residential floor plan (left)
Erdgeschoss (oben links)
Grundriss Regelgeschosse Büro (oben rechts)
Grundriss Regelgeschosse Wohnen (links)

Europe's first intersection with high-rise buildings taller than 100 meters at all four corners.
Europas erste Straßenkreuzung, die an allen vier Ecken Hochhäuser mit mehr als 100 Meter Höhe aufweist.

Jury statement:

The Omniturm Tower provides Frankfurt City with an elegant, modern and yet cheerful personality, greatly improving the urban resilience of the neighborhood. (Benjamin Romano)

According to Victor Stoltenburg & Horst R. Muth, the Omniturm high-rise stands for a completely new, future-oriented concept throughout Germany: *mixed-use*, i.e. several types of use in one high-rise building to achieve a lively mix. In the design of the tower, the 'swing' in the middle section—the residential area—stands out, creating interesting terrace concepts. In addition, the building convinces with its efficient division of space and functionality.

For Ina Hartwig, the Omniturm in Frankfurt lives up to its name. As the first true hybrid high-rise in Germany, it combines catering, offices, apartments, and shops under one roof. The mix is reflected in the archi-tecture in an elegant, playful way: the 'hip-swing' provides apartments, while the straight-lined sections of the tower accommodate offices. This puts it at the forefront of contemporary develop-ments in international urban planning comparison.

Jurystatement:

Der Omniturm ergänzt die Frankfurter Innenstadt um eine elegante, moderne und doch fröhliche Persön-lichkeit, die die urbane Resilienz des Quartiers deutlich verbessert. (Benjamin Romano)

Der Omniturm, so Victor Stoltenburg und Horst R. Muth, steht für ein deutschlandweit völlig neues, zukunft-weisendes Konzept: „mixed-use", also mehrere Nutzungsarten in einem Hochhaus, um eine lebendige Durchmischung zu erreichen. Beim Design des Turms sticht der „Schwung" im Mittelteil – dem Wohnbereich – heraus, wodurch interessante Terrassenkonzepte entstehen. Darüber hinaus überzeugt das Gebäude durch seine effiziente Flächenaufteilung und Funktionalität.

Für Ina Hartwig macht der Omniturm in Frankfurt seinem Namen alle Ehre. Als erstes echtes Hybridhochhaus in Deutschland vereint er Gastronomie, Büros, Wohnungen und Geschäfte unter einem Dach. Die Durchmischung spiegelt sich in der Architektur auf elegante, spielerische Weise wider: Im „Hüftschwung" wird gewohnt, die geradlinigen Abschnitte des Gebäudes beherbergen Büros. Damit ist es im internationalen städtebaulichen Vergleich auf der Höhe der Zeit.

Finalist 2020

Heatherwick Studio
EDEN
Singapore Singapur

Architects Architekten **Heatherwick Studio, London, UK** Großbritannien

Architects of record Lokale Architekten **RSP Architects Planners & Engineers**
Client Bauherr **Swire Properties, Celestial Fortune**
Structural engineers Tragwerksplanung **RSP Structures**
MEP Haustechnik **Squire Mech Pte Ltd.**

Height Höhe **105 m**
Stories Geschosse **20**

Site area Grundstücksfläche **3105 m²**
Building footprint Bebaute Fläche **300 m²**
Gross floor area Bruttogeschossfläche **6521 m²**
Structure Konstruktion **Reinforced concrete** Stahlbeton
Completion Fertigstellung **December** Dezember **2019**
Main use Hauptnutzung **Residential** Wohnen

Sustainability:
Green Mark Platinum certification; elaborate greening; cross-ventilation eliminates the need for electronic air conditioning

Nachhaltigkeit:
Green-Mark-Zertifizierung in Platin; aufwendige Begrünung; aufgrund von Querlüftung kann auf elektronische Klimatisierung verzichtet werden

The concrete elements and the lushly planted balconies provide the shading necessary for the tropics.
Die Betonelemente und die üppig bepflanzten Balkone sorgen für die in den Tropen notwendige Verschattung.

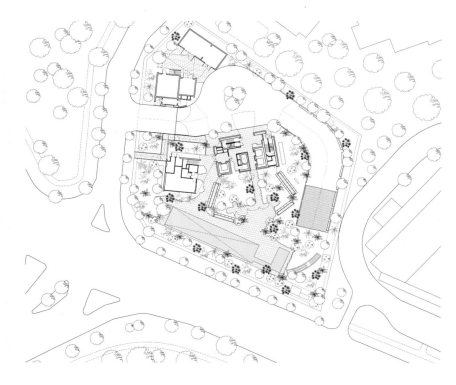

Site plan
Lageplan

Based on Singapore's urban development concept of a *City in a Garden*, EDEN combines high-class apartments with closeness to nature in the central and very popular District 10. In the middle of an exclusive neighborhood, the building literally elevates Singapore's species-rich landscape.

The 20 apartments, all of which have a living space of 282 square meters and a ceiling height of three meters, each extend over an entire floor. Around a large, column-free living room with an adjacent main balcony, the remaining rooms are grouped in three concrete elements. These peripheral cores extend across the entire height of the building, simultaneously providing the supporting structure of the residential tower. Their external surfaces are finished with a brown, three-dimensional texture representing an abstract image of Singapore's topography. This lends the material an organic look, and the appearance of the building varies with changing light.

More than 20 native plants grow in the integrated planters.
Mehr als 20 heimische Pflanzen wachsen in den integrierten Pflanzkübeln.

Between the concrete elements there are balconies with integrated and generously planted shell-shaped planters, which were partly hand-made by local manufacturers. This arrangement of the building volume allows extensive cross-ventilation, which makes electronic air conditioning redundant. Folding balcony doors create a flowing transition between interior and exterior. This impression is reinforced by the fact that the floor covering of the living areas, although different in material, hardly differs visually from that of the balconies, which are up to 15 meters long. The lush greenery comprising more than twenty tropical plant species, which were extensively researched for this project, completes the feeling of living in a tropical jungle.

The concrete elements together with the planters (a combination reminiscent of the Hive—NTU Learning Hub for the University of Singapore, also designed by Heatherwick Studio) provide shading that is necessary in the tropics and ensure privacy. At the same time, they afford exclusive views and sufficient natural lighting.

The prevailing materials used for the interior fittings —solid wood, limed concrete, and slate—continue the tactile, nature-oriented concept.

At the foot of the tower is an open, 18-meter high entrance hall, which is also flooded with light and air. Here, the green of the communal garden with a large pool leads inside the building. Another communal garden for the residents is located on the rooftop.

Basierend auf Singapurs Stadtentwicklungskonzept „City in a Garden" vereint EDEN im zentralen und gefragten District 10 hochklassiges Wohnen mit Naturnähe. Inmitten einer exklusiven Nachbarschaft verlagert das Gebäude die artenreiche Landschaft Singapurs buchstäblich in die Höhe.

Die insgesamt 20 Wohnungen, jede mit einer Wohnfläche von 282 Quadratmetern und einer Raumhöhe von drei Metern, erstrecken sich über jeweils eine ganze Etage. Um ein großes, stützenfreies Wohnzimmer mit anschließendem Hauptbalkon gruppieren sich die übrigen Räume in drei Betonelemente. Diese außenliegenden Kerne erstrecken sich über die gesamte Gebäudehöhe und bilden zugleich die Tragstruktur des Wohnturms. Ihre Außenflächen sind von dreidimensionaler, in Braun gehaltener Textur und repräsentieren ein abstrahiertes Abbild der Topografie Singapurs. Dadurch wirkt das Material organisch und die Erscheinung des Gebäudes verändert sich mit wechselndem Licht.

Zwischen den Betonelementen befinden sich Balkone mit üppig bepflanzten, integrierten muschelförmigen Pflanzkübeln, die von lokalen Herstellern teilweise in Handarbeit produziert wurden. Diese Anordnung der Baumasse ermöglicht extensive Querlüftung, weshalb auf elektronische Klimatisierung verzichtet werden kann. Faltbare Balkontüren erzeugen einen fließenden Übergang zwischen Innen und Außen. Dass sich der Bodenbelag der Wohnräume zwar im Material, aber optisch kaum vom Belag der bis zu 15 Meter langen Balkone unterscheidet, verstärkt diesen Eindruck. Die üppige Begrünung mit mehr als 20 tropischen Pflanzenarten, die aufwendig für dieses Projekt recherchiert wurden, komplettiert das Gefühl des Wohnens im tropischen Dschungel.

Die Betonelemente wie auch die Pflanzkübel (eine Kombination, die an das ebenfalls von Heatherwick Studio entworfene Hive – NTU Learning Hub für die Universität Singapur erinnert) sorgen für die in den Tropen notwendige Verschattung und bieten Schutz vor unerwünschten Einblicken. Gleichzeitig gewähren sie exklusive Ausblicke und ausreichend natürliche Belichtung.

Bei der Innenausstattung setzen die vorherrschenden Materialien Massivholz, gekalkter Beton und Schiefer das taktile naturnahe Konzept fort.

Am Fuß des Hochhauses befindet sich eine 18 Meter hohe, offene Eingangshalle, die ebenfalls von Licht und Luft durchflutet wird. Hier leitet das Grün des gemeinschaftlichen Gartens mit großem Pool in das Innere des Gebäudes über. Ein weiterer Gemeinschaftsgarten für die Bewohner befindet sich auf dem Dach.

The peripheral concrete elements and cores provide the supporting structure of the tower.
Die außenliegenden Betonelemente und Kerne bilden die Tragstruktur des Wohnturms.

On each floor there is only one apartment, which offers sheltered balconies in all directions.
In jedem Geschoss befindet sich nur eine Wohnung, die geschützte Balkone in alle Richtungen bietet.

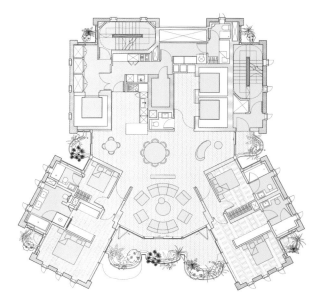

Floor Plan Apartments
Grundriss Wohnungen

Jury statement:

Klaus Fäth perceives the positive greening concept as a 'Garden of Eden', which protects the plants by means of recessed balconies and projecting walls.

The EDEN has an almost lascivious and sensually baroque aura. From the bulbous shell motifs and green jungle emanates a great power and attraction, which you cannot escape—it is an architectural seduction to dare something. (Anett-Maud Joppien)

For Peter Cachola Schmal, EDEN is a neo-baroque green icon in the self-proclaimed *City in a Garden*, which rethinks living in stacked up villas in the vertical direction and stages life without air conditioning as a model.

Jurystatement:

Als „Garten Eden" empfindet Klaus Fäth das positive Begrünungskonzept, bei dem die Pflanzen durch die zurückspringenden Balkone und vorspringende Wandscheiben geschützt werden.

Das EDEN hat eine fast laszive und sinnlich-barocke Aura. Von den bauchigen Muschelmotiven und dem grünen Urwald geht eine große Macht und Anziehungskraft aus, der man sich nicht entziehen kann – eine architektonische Verführung, etwas zu wagen. (Anett-Maud Joppien)

Für Peter Cachola Schmal ist EDEN eine neobarocke Grün-Ikone in der selbstproklamierten „City in a Garden", welche das gestapelte Villenwohnen in der Vertikalen neu denkt und ein Leben ohne Klimaanlage als Vorbild inszeniert.

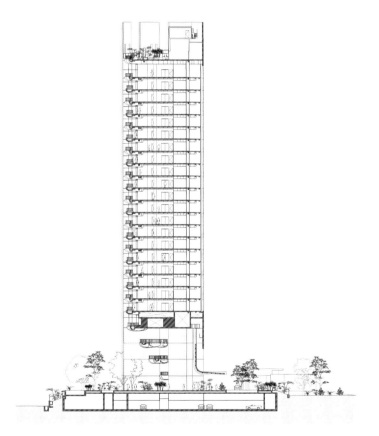

Section
Schnitt

Finalist 2020

Skidmore, Owings & Merrill LLP
THE STRATFORD
London, United Kingdom Großbritannien

Architects Architekten **Skidmore, Owings & Merrill LLP, London, UK** Großbritannien
Project architects Projektarchitekten **Kent Jackson, Phil Obayda, Julia Skeete, Chistopher Wollaston**
Client Bauherr **Manhattan Loft Corporation**
Structural engineers Tragwerksplanung **Skidmore, Owings & Merrill LLP**
MEP Haustechnik **Hoare Lea**

Height Höhe **143 m**
Stories Geschosse **42**
Site area Grundstücksfläche **2500 m²**
Building footprint Bebaute Fläche **1800 m²**
Gross floor area Bruttogeschossfläche **37 840 m²**
Structure Konstruktion **Reinforced concrete with steel** Stahlbeton und Stahl
Completion Fertigstellung **October** Oktober **2019**
Main use Hauptnutzung **Mixed use comprising hotel, gastronomy and apartments** Mischnutzung aus Hotel, Gastronomie und Wohnen

Sustainability:
excellent connections to local public transport to promote a car-free lifestyle; integrated into district-wide heating network; envelope comprises of an innovative high-performance serrated façade that prioritizes passive measures to minimize solar gains and optimize natural ventilation; sky gardens create a total green cover that is larger than the site area, so the project has a net positive impact on biodiversity

Nachhaltigkeit:
hervorragende Anbindung an den öffentlichen Nahverkehr zur Förderung eines autofreien Lebensstils; Integration in ein flächendeckendes Fernwärmenetz; die Gebäudehülle besteht aus einer innovativen, sägezahnartigen Hochleistungsfassade, die vor allem passive Maßnahmen zur Minimierung der Solareinträge und Optimierung der natürlichen Belüftung nutzt; Sky Gardens bilden eine Grünfläche, die zusammengenommen größer ist als die Grundstücksfläche, sodass das Projekt insgesamt positive Auswirkungen auf die Biodiversität hat

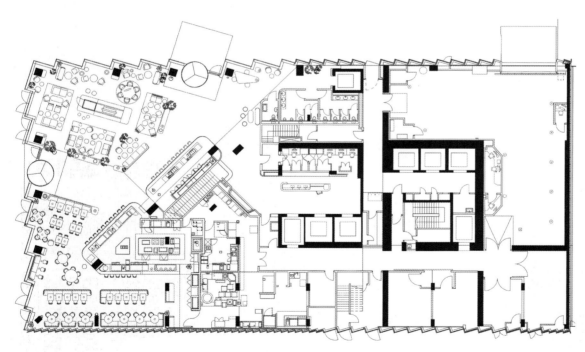

The diagonal division makes the upper part of the tower almost look like a gigantic advertising sign.
Die diagonale Teilung lässt den oberen Teil des Turms fast wie ein gigantisches Werbeschild erscheinen.

Ground floor plan
Grundriss Erdgeschoss

Three deep incisions characterize the shape of the tower and form roof terraces.
Drei tiefe Einschnitte prägen die Form des Turms und bilden Dachterrassen aus.

The Stratford is located in the district of the same name, which is currently still unknown to non-Londoners, but is one of the fastest growing and most diverse neighborhoods in the capital city. In the immediate vicinity is the Queen Elizabeth Olympic Park, where the 2012 Olympic Games were held. Since 2018, the University College London has also operated a branch here, as will the Victoria & Albert Museum from 2023, which is currently implementing not only a new museum building but also a large research and collection center together with the Smithsonian Institute. With its largest new building project to date, project developer Manhattan Loft Corporation is again focusing on the future development of a previously unknown part of London.

At first sight, the tower with the huge billboard might not be located in London but in Las Vegas. However, upon closer examination, one recognizes that this is not a superimposed advertising sign. Rather, the square tower is diagonally divided and recessed at the top. This creates space for a triangular, jointly used terrace. The same applies to the deep recesses at the transition from the plinth to the tower and about half way up the tower. They are made possible by the ingenious supporting structure using a steel belt truss system at level 10 and 28.

These floors were not designed to accommodate building technology in order to discreetly conceal the supporting structure; instead, exclusive apartments are located here, inside which the visible steel girders in combination with the raw concrete walls create an 'industrial loft' atmosphere. Tenants can choose from a total of 60 different types of apartments, ranging from one-room studios with 40 square meters to two-story maisonettes and spacious four-room penthouses with a floor area of 120 square meters.

The unconventional shape is enveloped by a pleated façade, which makes the building shimmer depending on the viewing angle. When looking from above, it becomes clear that these are not shading elements, but that the façade has actually been folded countless times.

The mixed use comprising a design hotel, condominiums, and short-term accommodation is intended to combine the privacy of one's private apartment with the comfort of a hotel. The Stratford wants to tie in with an era when celebrities such as Coco Chanel, Oscar Wilde, and Bob Dylan not only spent a night in a great hotel but lived there, thus making the location a meeting place not only for its occupants, but also for local residents.

The Stratford liegt im derzeit für Nicht-Londoner noch unbekannten Stadtteil gleichen Namens, der jedoch zu den am schnellsten wachsenden und vielfältigsten gehört. In unmittelbarer Nähe befindet sich der Queen Elizabeth Olympic Park, wo die Olympischen Spiele 2012 stattfanden. Seit 2018 hat das University College London hier ebenso einen Ableger wie ab 2023 das Victoria & Albert Museum, das derzeit nicht nur einen neuen Museumsbau, sondern auch ein großes Forschungs- und Sammlungszentrum gemeinsam mit dem Smithsonian Institut verwirklicht. Der Projektentwickler Manhattan Loft Corporation setzt mit seinem bisher größten Neubauprojekt einmal mehr auf die zukünftige Entwicklung eines bislang unbekannten Stadtteils Londons.

Auf den ersten Blick mag man den Turm mit dem riesigen Billboard nicht in London, sondern in Las Vegas verorten. Bei genauerer Betrachtung erkennt man jedoch, dass es sich hier nicht um ein aufgesetztes Werbeschild handelt. Vielmehr ist der quadratische Turm an seiner Spitze diagonal geteilt und springt zurück. So entsteht Raum für eine dreieckige, gemeinschaftlich genutzte Terrasse. Gleiches gilt für die tiefen Einschnitte am Übergang vom Sockelbau zum Turm und auf etwa halber Höhe des Turms. Ermöglicht werden sie durch das ausgeklügelte Tragwerk mit offen liegendem Stahlfachwerk im 10. und 28. Stockwerk.

In diesen Stockwerken wurden nicht etwa Technikgeschosse untergebracht, um das Tragwerk verschämt zu verbergen, sondern auch hier befinden sich exklusive Wohnungen, in denen durch die sichtbaren Stahlträger in Kombination mit den rohen Betonwänden „Industrial Loft"-Atmosphäre entsteht. Insgesamt haben die Mieter die Wahl zwischen 60 verschiedenen Wohnungstypen, vom Einzimmerapartment mit 40 Quadratmetern über zweigeschossige Maisonette-Wohnungen bis hin zum großzügigen Vier-Zimmer-Penthouse mit 120 Quadratmetern.

Ummantelt wird die eigenwillige Form von einer in Plisseefalten gelegten Fassade, die den Bau je nach Blickwinkel changieren lässt. Beim Blick von oben wird klar, dass es sich dabei nicht um vorgehängte Verschattungselemente handelt, sondern die Fassade tatsächlich in unzählige Falten gelegt ist.

Die Nutzungsmischung aus Designhotel, Eigentumswohnungen und Wohnungen auf Zeit soll die Privatsphäre einer eigenen Wohnung mit dem Komfort eines Hotels verbinden. The Stratford möchte damit an eine Ära anknüpfen, in der Berühmtheiten wie Coco Chanel, Oscar Wilde oder Bob Dylan nicht nur eine Nacht in einem großartigen Hotel verbrachten, sondern dort lebten und den Ort auf diese Weise zum Treffpunkt nicht nur seiner Bewohner, sondern auch der Anwohner machten.

Lobby
Eingangshalle

The ingenious supporting structure
using a steel belt truss on the 10th
and 28th floors allows for deep cuts
and is displayed in the apartments in
question.
Das ausgeklügelte Tragwerk mit
offenliegendem Stahlfachwerk im 10. und
28. Stockwerk ermöglicht die tiefen
Einschnitte und wird in den betreffenden
Wohnungen zur Schau gestellt.

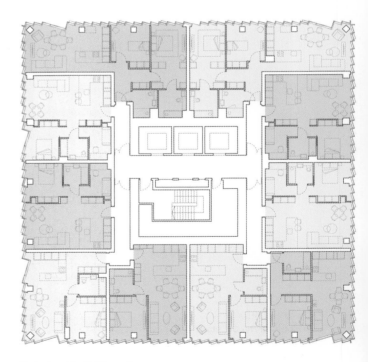

Typical residential floor plan
Wohnungsgrundrisse Regelgeschoss

Jury statement:

The *mixed-use* tower constructed in East London directly adjacent to the Olympic Park is revitalizing the district and offering a new residential concept. With the recesses in the building, the distinctive architecture features green rest areas, creating more green spaces than the base area covers. Finally, Victor Stoltenburg & Horst R. Muth are also convinced by the excellent public transport connections to two important railway stations as an essential component of the building's sustainability.

The spatiality created by double and single ceiling heights throughout the building, its greened and cantilever public spaces, and the meticulous solid and translucid design of the envelope make for a state-of-the-art high-rise building that inspires Benjamín Romano.

The deep, terrace-like incisions in the silhouette of the tower significantly reduce wind development and thus have a positive influence on wind comfort at pedestrian level. (Rudi Scheuermann)

Jurystatement:

Das im Osten Londons errichtete „mixed-use"-Hochhaus unmittelbar am Olympiapark belebt den Stadtteil und bietet ein neues Wohnkonzept an. Die unverwechselbare Architektur verfügt mit den Einschnitten in das Gebäude über grüne Ruhezonen; so entstehen mehr Grünflächen, als in der Grundfläche bebaut wurden. Schließlich überzeugt Victor Stoltenburg und Horst R. Muth auch der hervorragende ÖPNV-Anschluss an zwei wichtige Bahnhöfe als wesentlicher Baustein für die Nachhaltigkeit des Gebäudes.

Die Räumlichkeit, die durch doppelte und einfache Raumhöhen im gesamten Gebäude geschaffen wird, seine begrünten und freitragenden öffentlichen Räume und die sorgfältige massive und transluzide Gestaltung der Hülle ergeben ein modernstes Hochhaus, das Benjamín Romano inspiriert.

Die tiefen terrassenartigen Einschnitte entlang der Hochhaussilhouette reduzieren die Windentwicklung deutlich und haben somit einen positiven Einfluss auf den Windkomfort auf Fußgängerniveau.
(Rudi Scheuermann)

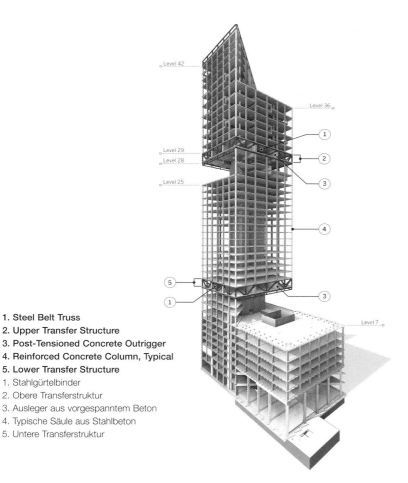

1. Steel Belt Truss
2. Upper Transfer Structure
3. Post-Tensioned Concrete Outrigger
4. Reinforced Concrete Column, Typical
5. Lower Transfer Structure

1. Stahlgürtelbinder
2. Obere Transferstruktur
3. Ausleger aus vorgespanntem Beton
4. Typische Säule aus Stahlbeton
5. Untere Transferstruktur

Finalist 2020

Zaha Hadid Architects
LEEZA SOHO
Beijing Peking, **China**

Architects Architekten **Zaha Hadid Architects,
London, UK** Großbritannien
Project architects Projektarchitekten **Zaha Hadid;
Patrik Schumacher; Satoshi Ohashi; Kaloyan
Erevinov; Ed Gaskin, Armando Solano; Philipp
Ostermaier**
Architects of record Lokale Architekten **Beijing
Institute of Architectural Design**
Client Bauherr **SOHO China Ltd.**
Structural engineers Tragwerksplanung **Bollinger +
Grohmann, China Academy of Building Research,
Beijing Institute of Architectural Design**
MEP Haustechnik **Parsons Brinkerhoff, Beijing
Institute of Architectural Design**

Height Höhe **200 m**
Stories Geschosse **45**
Site area Grundstücksfläche **14 365 m²**
Building footprint Bebaute Fläche **2488 m²**
Gross floor area Bruttogeschossfläche **172 800 m²**
Structure Konstruktion **Concrete and steel**
Beton und Stahl
Completion Fertigstellung **November 2019**
Main use Hauptnutzung **Office** Büros

Sustainability:
LEED Gold certification; advanced 3D BIM energy
management; heat recovery from exhaust air and
high-efficiency pumps, fans, chillers, boilers, lighting,
and controls; water collection, low-flow rate fixtures,
and graywater flushing; insulating green roof with
photovoltaic array to harvest solar energy; 2680
bicycle parking spaces; dedicated charging spaces
for electric and hybrid cars; low content of volatile
organic compound materials to minimize interior
pollutants; high-efficiency filters remove particulates
via the air-handling system

Nachhaltigkeit:
LEED-Gold-Zertifizierung; fortschrittliches 3D-BIM-
Energiemanagement; Wärmerückgewinnung aus Abluft
und hocheffiziente Pumpen, Ventilatoren, Kühlanlagen,
Heizkessel, Beleuchtung und Steuerungen; Wasser-
sammlung, Armaturen mit niedriger Durchflussrate und
Toilettenspülung mit Grauwasser; isolierendes begrüntes
Dach mit Photovoltaikanlage zur Gewinnung von Solar-
energie; 2680 Fahrradstellplätze; Ladesäulen für
Elektro- und Hybridautos; geringer Gehalt an flüchtigen
organischen Verbindungen zur Minimierung von Schad-
stoffen im Innenraum; Hochleistungsfilter entfernen
Partikel über das Belüftungssystem

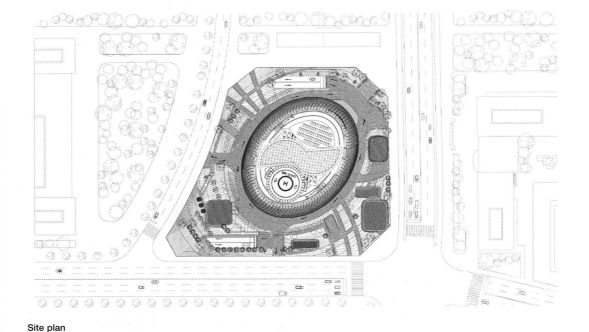

Site plan
Lageplan

The building volume
is divided into two
halves, each with its
own structural core
with external columns
and a steel tension
ring following the
tower's curved
outside structure.
Das Volumen des
Hochhauses ist in zwei
Hälften geteilt. Jede
der beiden Hälften hat
einen eigenen
strukturellen Kern mit
außenliegenden
Stützen und
stählernem Zugring,
der der gekurvten
Außenstruktur des
Turms folgt.

Four sky bridges
connect the two
halves of the tower.
Vier Brücken verbinden
die beiden Turmhälften
miteinander.

The scale-like glass
modules of the
façade have
ventilation fields on
the sides for efficient
room ventilation.
Die schuppenartigen
Glasmodule der
Fassade weisen an den
Seiten Belüftungsfelder
zur effizienten
Raumbelüftung auf.

The 45-story Leeza SOHO tower provides flexible office space for small and medium-sized enterprises and is the center of the new Fengtai business district, a growing financial and transport hub not far from the recently opened Beijing Daxing International Airport in southwest Beijing.

Due to its proximity to the local railway station, the tower is, on the one hand, optimally connected to the city's public transport network, while, on the other hand, a subway line runs directly underneath the tower, diagonally dissecting it on the fourth basement level. This had a lasting influence on the design of Leeza Soho and is the reason why the building volume is divided into two halves, each with its own structural core with external columns and a steel tension ring following the tower's curved outside structure. The combination of a reinforced concrete structure for the tower halves and a supporting steel structure for the connecting bridges enables the curved building shape, while at the same time ensuring structural and economic feasibility.

The 194.15-meter high atrium of Leeza SOHO is the tallest in the world and serves as a public space for the district. Rotating dynamically by 45 degrees, it divides the building over its full height into two halves that are connected by four sky bridges. These bridges along the curved exterior shell are built of steel trussed girders and provide resistance to bending stresses.

The sculptural division brings natural light deep into the building and offers views both across the city and into the atrium. The void acts as a thermal chimney that additionally regulates the indoor climate. In combination with the internal ventilation system, this ensures an effective air purification process. Due to their rotation, the two halves of the tower shade the atrium and, in combination with the double-insulated low-e glazing, maintain a pleasant indoor climate.

The glazing envelops the entire building with a modular curtain wall whose elements are staggered like scales and have narrow ventilation strips at the sides. If necessary, air is drawn in through these cavities to provide efficient room ventilation. The thermal envelope protects against the extreme temperatures in the Chinese metropolis. Moreover, the office building is equipped with a green roof and a photovoltaic array, and it is surrounded by a public square that reflects the curved shape of the tower.

Der 45 Stockwerke hohe Turm Leeza SOHO bietet flexible Büroflächen für kleine und mittlere Unternehmen und ist Zentrum des neuen Fengtai-Geschäftsviertels, ein wachsendes Finanz- und Mobilitätszentrum unweit des kürzlich eröffneten Beijing Daxing International Airport im Südwesten Beijings.

Aufgrund der Nähe zum lokalen Bahnhof ist der Turm zum einen optimal an das Nahverkehrsnetz der Stadt angeschlossen, zum anderen verläuft deshalb direkt unter dem Turm eine U-Bahn-Strecke, welche ihn im vierten Untergeschoss diagonal teilt. Dies beeinflusste das Design des Leeza SOHO Turms nachhaltig und ist der Grund dafür, dass das Volumen des Hochhauses in zwei Hälften geteilt ist. Jede der beiden Hälften hat einen eigenen strukturellen Kern mit außenliegenden Stützen und stählernem Zugring, der der gekurvten Außenstruktur des Turms folgt. Die Kombination der Konstruktion aus Stahlbeton für die Turmhälften und Stahltragwerk für die verbindenden Brücken ermöglicht die geschwungene Gebäudeform bei gleichzeitiger konstruktiver und ökonomischer Realisierbarkeit.

Das 194,15 Meter hohe Atrium des Leeza SOHO ist das höchste der Welt und dient als öffentlicher Raum für das Viertel. Dynamisch um 45 Grad rotierend, teilt es das Gebäude auf ganzer Höhe in zwei Bereiche, die über Brücken miteinander verbunden sind. Die vier Brücken entlang der geschwungenen Außenhülle, die die Türme verbinden, bestehen aus Stahlfachwerkträgern und bieten Widerstand gegen Biegebeanspruchungen.

Die skulpturale Teilung lässt natürliches Licht bis tief in das Gebäude hinein und bietet neben Ausblicken über die Stadt und ins Atrium auch den Vorteil eines thermischen Schornsteins, der das Raumklima zusätzlich reguliert. In Verbindung mit dem internen Belüftungssystem sorgt dies für einen effektiven Luftreinigungsprozess. Die beiden Turmhälften verschatten durch ihre Drehung das Atrium und sorgen in Kombination mit der Doppelisolierverglasung mit niedrigem Emissionsgrad für ein angenehmes Innenklima.

Die Verglasung umschließt das gesamte Gebäude mit einer modularen Vorhangfassade, deren Elemente schuppenartig versetzt sind und an den Seiten schmale Belüftungsfelder aufweisen. Durch diese wird bei Bedarf Luft zur effizienten Raumbelüftung eingezogen. Die thermische Hülle schützt vor den extremen Temperaturen in der chinesischen Metropole. Das Bürogebäude ist zudem mit einem begrünten Dach und Photovoltaikanlagen ausgestattet und wird von einem öffentlichen Platz umgeben, der die runde Gestalt des Turms widerspiegelt.

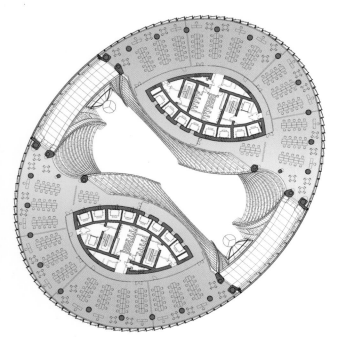

Typical floor plan
Regelgrundriss

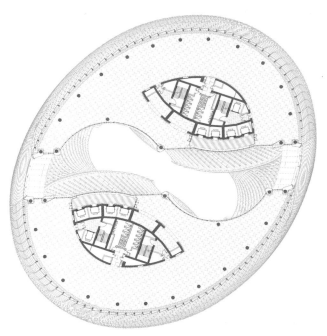

Floor plan level 40
Grundriss 40. Obergeschoss

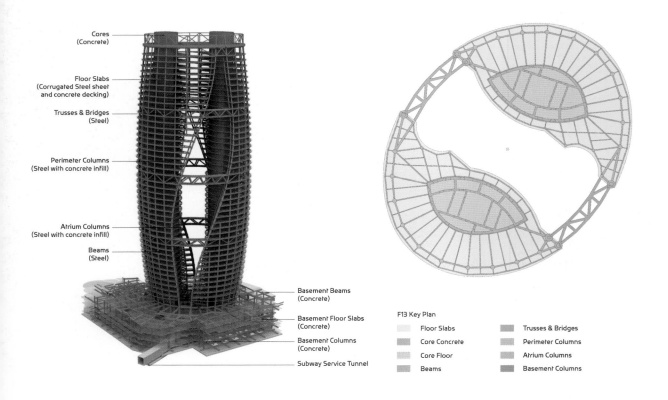

Cores
(Concrete)

Floor Slabs
(Corrugated Steel sheet
and concrete decking)

Trusses & Bridges
(Steel)

Perimeter Columns
(Steel with concrete infill)

Atrium Columns
(Steel with concrete infill)

Beams
(Steel)

Basement Beams
(Concrete)

Basement Floor Slabs
(Concrete)

Basement Columns
(Concrete)

Subway Service Tunnel

F13 Key Plan

Floor Slabs		Trusses & Bridges	
Core Concrete		Perimeter Columns	
Core Floor		Atrium Columns	
Beams		Basement Columns	

Jury statements:

Breath-taking is Andreas Moser´s description of the twin tower in a wonderful, parametrically designed glass bubble with a lot of air in between.
— Spaceship on earth

Dizziness seizes me as I enter the large atrium, but immediately I grow wings and take off for a flight, Anett-Maud Joppien describes her impressions.

For Peter Cachola Schmal, Leeza SOHO is the sculptural solution for a twin tower block that focuses on creating spatially overwhelming impressions and experiences for hundreds of small offices and home offices that take up their digital quarters on the way to the new airport.

Rudi Scheuermann explains:
The façade is structured as a scale-like, parametrically arranged element façade in a way that it provides the eye with a target that is perceived favorably, especially when moving around the building. The superstructure, which connects the two towers via the atrium, gives the high-rise the greatest possible resilience in terms of mutual structural bracing.

Jurystatements:

Atemberaubend findet Andreas Moser den Doppelturm, in einer wunderbar parametrisch gestalteten Glasblase mit einer Menge Luft dazwischen.
– Spaceship on earth

Schwindel überkommt mich, als ich das große Atrium betrete, aber sofort wachsen mir Flügel und ich hebe ab, beschreibt Anett-Maud Joppien ihre Eindrücke.

Für Peter Cachola Schmal ist das Leeza SOHO die skulpturale Lösung eines Doppelhochhauses, das auf räumliche Überwältigung und Erlebnisse setzt für Hunderte von Small Offices und Homeoffices, die auf dem Weg zum neuen Flughafen ihr digitales Quartier aufschlagen.

Rudi Scheuermann erklärt:
Die Fassade ist als schuppenartige, parametrisch verlaufende Elementfassade so strukturiert, dass sie dem Auge Angriffsfläche bietet, die vor allem beim Bewegen um das Gebäude wohlwollend wahrgenommen wird. Die Superstruktur, mit der die beiden Türme über das Atrium verbunden sind, gibt den Hochhäusern größtmögliche Resilienz bezüglich gegenseitiger statischer Aussteifung.

The 194.15-meter high atrium is the tallest in the world
Das Atrium ist mit 194,15 Metern das höchste der Welt.

Nominated Project 2020
Nominiertes Projekt 2020

Ateliers Jean Nouvel
LA MARSEILLAISE
Marseille, France Frankreich

Architects Architekten **Jean Nouvel – Ateliers Jean Nouvel, Paris, France** Frankreich
Project architects Projektarchitekten **Alain Gvozdenovic, Nathalie Sasso, Vincent Delfaud**
Architects of record Lokale Architekten **Tangram Architectes**
Client Bauherr **Constructa Urban System**
Structural engineers Tragwerksplanung **AEDIS, SIDF**
MEP Haustechnik **ALTO Ingénierie**

Height Höhe **135 m**
Stories Geschosse **31**
Site area Grundstücksfläche **2300 m²**
Building footprint Bebaute Fläche **1450 m²**
Gross floor area Bruttogeschossfläche **46 767 m²**
Structure Konstruktion **Concrete and steel** Beton und Stahl
Completion Fertigstellung **October** Oktober **2018**
Main use Hauptnutzung **Office** Büros

Sustainability:
pursuing "Excellent" HQE® and LEED Gold certification; connected to the Thassalia marine geothermal power station, which uses marine thermal energy to cool the building; eco-certified concretes as well as ultrahigh-performance fiber-reinforced concrete (UHPFRC); very well insulated; solar panels supply the restaurant; paint resistant to aging; improved acoustics thanks to absorbent spaces and energy recovery systems

Nachhaltigkeit:
strebt „Excellent" HQE® und LEED Gold Zertifizierung an; angeschlossen an das Geothermiekraftwerk Thassalia, das zur Kühlung des Gebäudes thermische Meeresenergie nutzt; öko-zertifizierte Betone sowie ultrahochleistungsfaserverstärkter Beton (UHPFRC); sehr gut isoliert; Sonnenkollektoren versorgen das Restaurant; Farbe alterungsbeständig; verbesserte Akustik durch absorbierende Räume und Energierückgewinnungssysteme

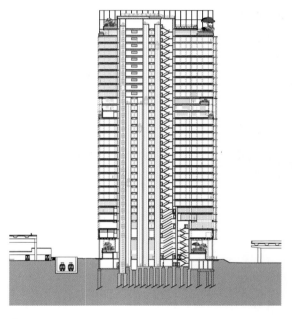

Section
Schnitt

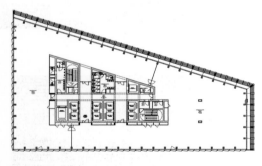

Typical floor plan
Grundriss Regelgeschoss

The architects of La Marseillaise aim at merging the building with the Mediterranean colors of Marseille. The grid-like façade design dissolves the separation between inside and outside by penetrating the glass front of the tower and continuing along the ceilings. The color scheme supports this effect. Thus red, white and blue determine the views both of and from the tower: the colors of the French national flag dissolve into the blue of the sky, the white of the clouds on the horizon, and the red of the surrounding tiled roofs. With its lightweight fiber-reinforced concrete structure and the delicacy of the envelope, the cuboid building shape creates a combination of simplicity and complexity. The external brise-soleil elements with their filigree, geometric shadows appear like a ladder to the sky.

Das Ziel der Architekten von La Marseillaise ist die Verschmelzung des Gebäudes mit den mediterranen Farben der Stadt Marseille. Die gitterartige Fassadenkonstruktion löst die Trennung von innen und außen auf, indem sie die Glasfront des Turmes durchdringt und sich entlang der Decken fortsetzt. Die Farbgebung unterstützt diesen Effekt. So bestimmen Rot, Weiß und Blau sowohl die Ansicht als auch die Aussicht: Die Farben der französische Nationalflagge gehen auf im Blau des Himmels, im Weiß der Wolken am Horizont und im Rot der umgebenden Ziegeldächer. Die quaderförmige Gebäudefigur schafft mit ihrer aus leichtem Faserbeton hergestellten Gebäudekonstruktion und der Feingliedrigkeit der Gebäudehülle eine Verbindung von Einfachheit und Komplexität. Die außen liegenden Brise Soleils mit ihren filigranen, geometrischen Schatten wirken wie eine Leiter in den Himmel.

Nominated Project 2020
Nominiertes Projekt 2020

Atkins
LANDMARK 81
Ho Chi Minh City Ho-Chi-Minh-Stadt, **Vietnam**

Architects Architekten **Atkins, Hong Kong** Hongkong, China
Project architects Projektarchitekten **Alex Peaker, Mai Quang Tri**
Client Bauherr **Vingroup**
Structural engineers Tragwerksplanung **Arup**
MEP Haustechnik **Aurecon**

Height Höhe **461 m**
Stories Geschosse **81**
Site area Grundstücksfläche **15 000 m²**
Building footprint Bebaute Fläche **8600 m²**

Gross floor area Bruttogeschossfläche **249 000 m²**
Structure Konstruktion **Composite construction** Verbundbauweise
Completion Fertigstellung **April 2019**
Main use Hauptnutzung **Mixed use comprising hotel, conference center, residential, retail, gastronomy** Mischnutzung aus Hotel, Konferenzräumen, Wohnen, Einzelhandel und Gastronomie

Sustainability:
highly efficient chiller system; HVAC system designed to meet green building standards; double glazed with low-e glass

Nachhaltigkeit:
hocheffizientes Kühlsystem; HLK-System zur Erfüllung der „Green Building Standards"; Doppelverglasung mit Low-E-Glas

Typical residential floor plan
Grundriss Regelgeschoss Wohnungen

Typical floor plan Hotel
Grundriss Regelgeschoss Hotel

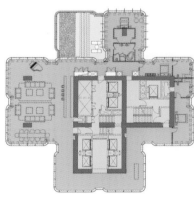

Floor plan Presidential Suite
Grundriss Präsidentensuite

A Vietnamese proverb says that "while a stick can be strong, a bundle of sticks will always be stronger." The logic of reinforced concrete construction complies with this metaphor of strength. Stiffening structural layers surround and strengthen the core of the tower. The building design is based on a pragmatic ground plan with a square core, each surrounded by six building sections. These are sculptured to reduce the core size, while supporting the iconic silhouette of the tower. The rounded corners emphasize the dynamic, soaring effect of the building. Situated directly on the Saigon River, Landmark 81 is Vietnam's tallest building and the nucleus of the Vinhomes Central Park urban development north of the city center.

Ein vietnamesisches Sprichwort besagt: „Ein Ast kann stark sein, ein Bündel von Ästen wird immer stärker sein." Dieser Metapher für Stärke folgt die Logik der Stahlbetonkonstruktion. Aussteifende Tragwerksschichten umschließen den Kern des Turms und stärken ihn. Der Gebäudeentwurf basiert auf einem pragmatischen Grundriss mit quadratischem Kern, umgeben von jeweils sechs Gebäudeteilen. Diese sind so gestaltet, dass sie die Kerngröße reduzieren und gleichzeitig die ikonische Figur des Turms unterstützen. Die abgerundeten Ecken unterstützen die dynamische, aufstrebende Wirkung des Gebäudes. Direkt am Saigon-Fluss gelegen, ist Landmark 81 Vietnams höchstes Gebäude und zugleich Nukleus der Stadtentwicklung des Vinhomes Central Park nördlich des Stadtzentrums.

Design Methodology
Entwurfsmethodik

Nominated Project 2020
Nominiertes Projekt 2020

BIG – Bjarke Ingels Group
SHENZHEN ENERGY HEADQUARTERS
Shenzhen, China

Architects Architekten **BIG – Bjarke Ingels Group,
Copenhagen** Kopenhagen/**New York, NY, Denmark**
Dänemark/**USA**
Project architects Projektarchitekten **Bjarke Ingels,
Andreas Klok Pedersen, Andre Schmidt, Martin
Voelkle**
Architects of record Lokale Architekten **Shenzhen
General Institute of Architectural Design and
Research**
Client Bauherr **Shenzhen Energy Company**
Structural engineers Tragwerksplanung **Arup**
MEP Haustechnik **Arup**

Height Höhe **218 m; 111 m**
Stories Geschosse **42; 19**
Site area Grundstücksfläche **10 400 m²**
Building footprint Bebaute Fläche **7200 m²**
Gross floor area Bruttogeschossfläche **142 590 m²**
Structure Konstruktion **Reinforced concrete
Stahlbeton**
Completion Fertigstellung **August 2018**
Main use Hauptnutzung **Office Büros**

Sustainability:
passive façade performance; maximum incidence
of daylight and minimum solar gain; glazed areas
take up approximately 20 percent of spandrel areas;
window-wall ratio of around 40 to 60; passive solar
heating

Nachhaltigkeit:
passive Fassadenleistung; maximaler Tageslichteinfall
und minimale Sonneneinstrahlung; verglaste Flächen
nehmen etwa 20 Prozent der Brüstungsflächen ein;
Fenster-Wand-Verhältnis von etwa 40 zu 60; passive
Solarheizung

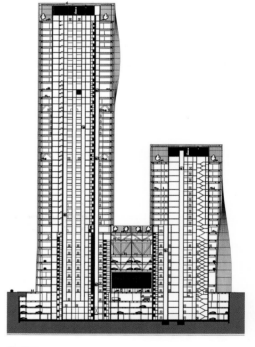

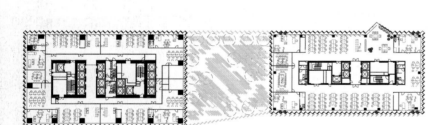

Typical floor plan
Grundriss Regelgeschoss

Section
Schnitt

The architects of the Shenzhen Energy
Headquarters focused on the façade to find a
sustainable solution for a contemporary tropical
modernism. In gentle waves, it envelops the two
towers with a rippled skin specially adapted to the
local climate. Folded parts of the building envelope
help reduce solar gains and glare caused by
sunlight. Their orientation corresponds to the course
of the sun—they open towards the north to let in
natural light, while the south side is protected from
intensive sunlight. The underlying idea is that by
implementing intelligent architecture, the energy
consumption of a building can be significantly
reduced, even without complicated building services
technology. A lateral supporting structure with
reinforced concrete cores and an external girder-
and-column grid protects the building against
typhoons and seismic activity.

Die Architekten der Firmenzentrale von Shenzhen
Energy konzentrierten sich auf die Fassade, um eine
nachhaltige Lösung für einen zeitgenössischen
tropischen Modernismus zu finden. In sanften Wellen
umschließt sie die beiden Türme mit einer geriffelten
Haut, die speziell an das lokale Klima angepasst wurde.
Die Faltungen der Gebäudehülle reduzieren Hitze-
einstrahlung und blendendes Sonnenlicht. Ihre
Ausrichtung korrespondiert mit dem Lauf der Sonne –
nach Norden öffnen sie sich, um natürliches Licht
hineinzulassen, während die Südseite vor dem starken
Sonnenlicht geschützt wird. Dahinter steht die Idee,
dass durch intelligente Architektur, auch ohne
komplizierte Gebäudetechnik, der Energieverbrauch
eines Gebäudes signifikant reduziert werden kann. Eine
laterale Tragstruktur mit Stahlbetonkernen und einem
externen Träger-und-Stützen-Raster schützt vor Taifunen
und seismischen Aktivitäten.

CCDI Group
SHENZHEN BAIDU HEADQUARTERS
Shenzhen, China

Architects Architekten **CCDI Group, Shenzhen, China**
Project architects Projektarchitekten **Zhaoming Wang,
Shining Yan**
Client Bauherr **Constructa Baidu Group**
Structural engineers Tragwerksplanung **CCDI Group,
SUP Ingenieure**
MEP Haustechnik **CCDI Group**

Height Höhe **189 m; 150 m**
Stories Geschosse **43; 33**
Site area Grundstücksfläche **14 000 m²**
Gross floor area Bruttogeschossfläche **226 000 m²**
Structure Konstruktion **Composite construction**
Verbundbauweise
Completion Fertigstellung **2018**
Main use Hauptnutzung **Office** Büros

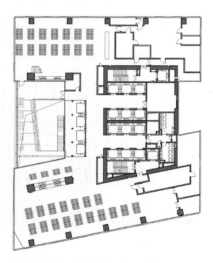

Floor plan level 14
Grundriss Geschoss 14

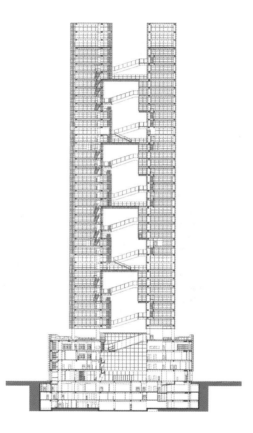

Section
Schnitt

The east and west façades of the two towers of the new Baidu Headquarters are broken up by spacious terraces every eight stories. External staircases connect individual levels at irregular intervals, thus forming a huge green 'zipper' that creates varied outdoor areas. Seating areas and greenery make the staircases themselves places of informal exchange as part of everyday working routines for the employees of one of China's leading Internet companies. The stairs are also part of the supporting structure, forming an inclined column between the floor slabs. Together with the multi-story platforms, they give structure and rhythm to the external appearance of the complex.

Die Ost- und Westfassaden der beiden Türme des neuen Baidu Headquarters werden alle acht Stockwerke von großzügigen Terrassen aufgebrochen. Ebenfalls im Freien liegende Treppen verbinden einzelne Stockwerke in unregelmäßigen Abständen miteinander und bilden so einen riesigen grünen „Reißverschluss", der abwechslungsreiche Außenbereiche bietet. Sitzbereiche und Begrünung machen auch die Treppen selbst zu Orten des informellen Austauschs im Arbeitsalltag der Angestellten einer der führenden Internetfirmen Chinas. Die Treppen sind zugleich Teil der Trag-struktur, sie bilden eine geneigte Stütze zwischen den Geschossdecken. Gemeinsam mit den Geschossübergreifenden Plattformen strukturieren und rhythmisieren sie die äußere Erscheinung des Komplexes.

Nominated Project 2020
Nominiertes Projekt 2020

CetraRuddy Architecture
ARO
New York, NY, USA

Architects Architekten **CetraRuddy Architecture, New York, NY, USA**
Project architects Projektarchitekten **John Cetra, Kevin Lee**
Client Bauherr **Algin Management**
Structural engineers Tragwerksplanung **Buro Happold, DeSimone Consulting Engineers**
MEP Haustechnik **Cosentini Associates**

Height Höhe **224 m**
Stories Geschosse **62**
Site area Grundstücksfläche **2712 m²**
Building footprint Bebaute Fläche **2712 m²**
Gross floor area Bruttogeschossfläche **50 168 m²**
Structure Konstruktion **Reinforced concrete** Stahlbeton
Completion Fertigstellung **September 2019**
Main use Hauptnutzung **Residential** Wohnen

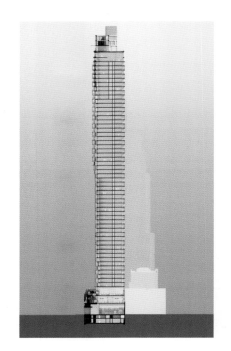

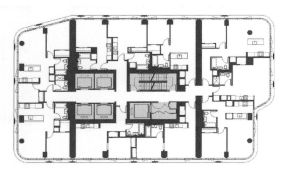

Typical floor plan lower level (smaller units)
Grundriss Regelgeschoss untere Ebenen (kleine Einheiten)

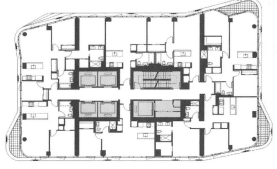

Typical floor plan upper level (larger units)
Grundriss Regelgeschoss obere Ebenen (gößere Einheiten)

In Manhattan's dense and vibrant theatre district, ARO makes a thoughtful contribution to urban living. The exterior shape was determined by the urban context and not least by numerous legal requirements, such as regulations on minimum distances from surrounding buildings. The elaborately detailed external façade grid is based on six modules, which allow numerous possible combinations and even develop into outdoor areas for some apartments at the corners of the building. The design of the horizontally laid out base area corresponds to the characteristic façade grid. Multi-level openings interrupt the horizontal structure in the interior and, together with generous green terraces, create opportunities for encounters.

Im dichten und lebendigen Theater District von Manhattan bietet ARO einen durchdachten Beitrag zum urbanen Wohnen. Die äußere Form wurde vom urbanen Kontext und nicht zuletzt von zahlreichen gesetzlichen Bestimmungen, wie zum Beispiel Abstandregeln zu den umgebenden Bauten, bestimmt. Das fein detaillierte äußere Fassadenraster ist aus sechs Modulen aufgebaut, die zahlreiche Kombinationsmöglichkeiten bieten und sich an den Ecken sogar zu Außenbereichen für einige Wohnungen entwickeln. Die Gestaltung des horizontal gelagerten Sockelbereichs korrespondiert mit dem prägenden Fassadenraster. Geschossübergreifende Öffnungen durchbrechen im Inneren die horizontale Gliederung und bieten gemeinsam mit großzügigen begrünten Terrassen Möglichkeiten der Begegnung.

Nominated Project 2020
Nominiertes Projekt 2020

Diller Scofidio + Renfro
15 HUDSON YARDS
New York, NY, USA

Architects Architekten **Diller Scofidio + Renfro, New York, NY, USA**
Project architects Projektarchitekten **Elizabeth Diller, Ricardo Scofidio, Charles Renfro, Benjamin Gilmartin, Robert Katchur**
Architect of record Lokale Architekten **Ismael Leyva Architects**
Client Bauherr **Related Properties**
Structural engineers Tragwerksplanung **WSP Cantor Seinuk**
MEP Haustechnik **JB&B (Jaros Baum & Bolles)**

Height Höhe **277 m**
Stories Geschosse **88**
Site area Grundstücksfläche **1360 m²**

Building footprint Bebaute Fläche **1040 m²**
Gross floor area Bruttogeschossfläche **91 070 m²**
Structure Konstruktion **Reinforced concrete** Stahlbeton
Completion Fertigstellung **February** Februar **2020**
Main use Hauptnutzung **Residential** Wohnen

Sustainability:
designed to meet LEED Gold certification; filtered fresh air; Lutron Home automation; grey water recycling system that uses storm water runoff to support cooling; microgrid and two cogeneration plants generate electricity

Nachhaltigkeit:
konzipiert, um LEED-Zertifizierung in Gold zu erhalten; gefilterte Frischluft; Hausautomation von Lutron; Grauwasser-Recyclinganlage, die den Regenwasser-abfluss zur Unterstützung der Gebäudekühlung nutzt; Microgrid und zwei Blockheizkraftwerke zur Strom-erzeugung

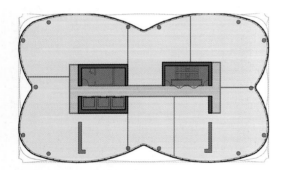

Floor plan residential level
Grundriss Wohngeschoss

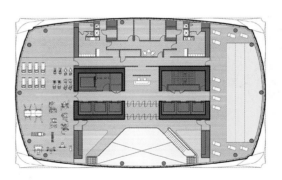

Floor plan amenity level
Grundriss Gemeinschaftseinrichtungen

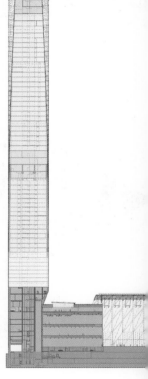

Section
Schnitt

Located directly adjacent to the High Line, the multi-purpose tower, together with New York's latest cultural center, The Shed, forms an ensemble in the new Hudson Yards high-rise cluster, which is supported by a platform spanning 30 active railroad tracks. The office and storage areas of the cultural center are located on the lower levels, while the residential tower rises above. Starting with an orthogonal ground plan, following the rigid grid of New York's streets, the floor plan morphs into a cloverleaf layout at the top, which affords panoramic views in various directions. North America's largest façade made of cold-bent glass is optimized to allow the filigree building shape while at the same time resisting high wind loads.

Direkt an der High-Line gelegen, bildet das funktions-gemischte Hochhaus gemeinsam mit New Yorks neuestem Kulturzentrum The Shed ein Ensemble im neuen Hochhauscluster der Hudson Yards, das auf einer 30 aktive Bahngleise überspannenden Plattform gründet. In den unteren Geschossen befinden sich die Büro- und Lagerflächen des Kulturzentrums, darüber erhebt sich der eigentliche Wohnturm. Zunächst auf einem orthogonalen Grundriss, dem rigiden New Yorker Straßenraster folgend, entwickelt sich die Grundfigur zu einer kleeblattförmigen Geschossfläche, die Aussichten in verschiedene Richtungen ermöglicht. Die größte Fassade Nordamerikas aus kalt gebogenem Glas ist so optimiert, dass sie einerseits die filigrane Gebäudeform erlaubt, zugleich aber auch den starken Windlasten widersteht.

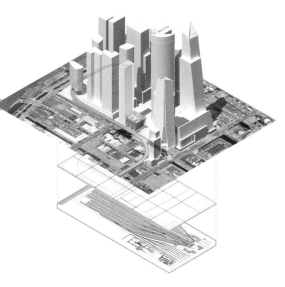

High Line Diagram
High-Line-Diagramm

Nominated Project 2020
Nominiertes Projekt 2020

Dominique Perrault Architecture
5th EXTENSION OF THE EUROPEAN COURT OF JUSTICE
Luxembourg, Luxembourg Luxemburg

Architects Architekten **Dominique Perrault Architecture, Paris, France** Frankreich
Project architect Projektarchitekt **David Agudo**
Architects of record Lokale Architekten **SRA Architects, Jean Petit Architects**
Client Bauherr **Administration of Public Buildings, Luxembourg**
Structural engineers Tragwerksplanung **Ney & Partners**
MEP Haustechnik **Felgen et Associes Engineering, Sorane**

Height Höhe **118 m**
Stories Geschosse **30**
Site area Grundstücksfläche **10 000 m²**
Building footprint Bebaute Fläche **4117 m²**
Gross floor area Bruttogeschossfläche **50 000 m²**

Structure Konstruktion **Reinforced concrete** Stahlbeton
Completion Fertigstellung **September 2019**
Main use Hauptnutzung **Office** Büros

Sustainability:
passive house standard class AAA, according to the Directive of the Grand Duchy of Luxembourg; 'excellent' rating according to BREEAM certification; mobile solar protection system; high-performance envelope and enhanced protection against cold; insulation (30 cm), combined with triple glazing; harnessing of heat from the data center for ventilation preheating and static night-time heating; solar thermal collectors; photovoltaic installation

Nachhaltigkeit:
Passivhausstandard der Klasse AAA nach der Richtlinie des Großherzogtums Luxemburg; BREEAM-Zertifikat „ausgezeichnet"; bewegliches Sonnenschutzsystem; leistungsstarke Gebäudehülle und erhöhter Kälteschutz; Isolierung (30 cm), kombiniert mit Dreifachverglasung; Nutzung der Abwärme des Rechenzentrums zur Vorwärmung der Belüftung und statischen Nachtheizung; thermische Solarkollektoren; Photovoltaikanlage

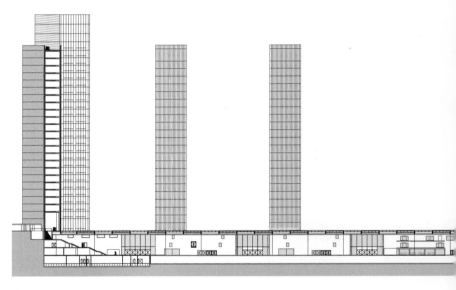

Ground floor plan Grundriss Erdgeschoss

Section Schnitt

The fifth extension completes the building complex for the European Court of Justice on the Kirchberg Plateau in Luxembourg. A large gallery, the 'backbone' of the ensemble, connects the new office tower directly to all the other buildings of the Court of Justice. Together with the podium, it follows the design continuity of its two neighbors, which were completed in 2008. Consisting of two slender, offset building slabs positioned next to each other, it exceeds them by six stories. The façade of the higher slab is made of the same black enameled glass as the actual courthouse. Analogous to the two other towers, the façade of the smaller slab is clad with golden modules, alternating between transparent and opaque.

Die fünfte Erweiterung vervollständigt den Gebäudekomplex für den Europäischen Gerichtshof auf dem Kirchberg-Plateau in Luxemburg. Über eine große Galerie, dem „Rückgrat" des Ensembles, ist der neue Büroturm direkt mit allen anderen Bauteilen des Gerichtshofs verbunden. Zusammen mit dem Sockelgebäude steht er in der gestalterischen Kontinuität seiner zwei Nachbarn, die bereits 2008 fertiggestellt wurden. Bestehend aus zwei dünnen, versetzt nebeneinander stehenden Scheiben überragt er diese jedoch um sechs Etagen. Die Fassade der höheren Scheibe ist aus dem gleichen schwarz emaillierten Glas wie die des eigentlichen Gerichtsgebäudes. Die Fassade der kleineren Scheibe ist analog zu den beiden anderen Türmen mit goldenen Modulen, im Wechsel transparent und opak, bekleidet.

Estudio de Arquitectura Alonso Balaguer
BACATÁ TOWER
Bogotá, Colombia Kolumbien

Architects Architekten **Estudio de Arquitectura Alonso Balaguer SLP, Barcelona, Spain** Spanien
Project architects Projektarchitekten **Sergio Balaguer; Luis Alonso; Javier Expósito**
Client Bauherr **BD PROMOTORES COLOMBIA SAS**
Structural engineers Tragwerksplanung **PYD Ingenieros**
MEP Haustechnik **Prabyc Ingenieros**

Height Höhe **216 m**
Stories Geschosse **67**
Site area Grundstücksfläche **4388 m²**
Building footprint Bebaute Fläche **3071 m²**

Gross floor area Bruttogeschossfläche **112 848 m²**
Structure Konstruktion **Reinforced concrete** Stahlbeton
Completion Fertigstellung **December** Dezember **2019**
Main use Hauptnutzung **Mixed use comprising residential, hotel, retail** Mischnutzung aus Wohnen, Hotel und Einzelhandel

Sustainability:
energy-efficient windows and glazing; natural ventilation in almost all areas; 40 percent of the terraces are green; energy-saving LED lighting; water-saving fittings; bicycle parking for all residents and visitors

Nachhaltigkeit:
energieeffiziente Fenster und Verglasung; natürliche Belüftung in nahezu allen Bereichen; 40 Prozent der Terrassen sind begrünt; energiesparende LED-Beleuchtung; wassersparende Armaturen; Fahrradparkplätze für alle Bewohner sowie Besucher

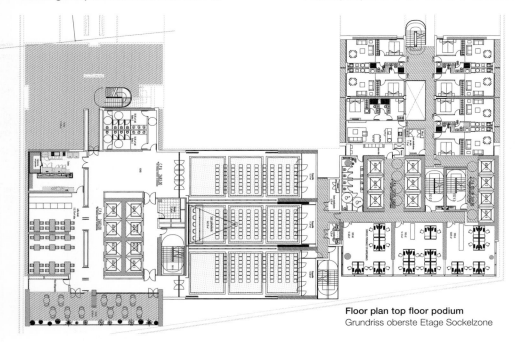

Floor plan top floor podium
Grundriss oberste Etage Sockelzone

Section
Schnitt

The Bacatá Tower is located in the heart of Bogotá, in close proximity to the historical center. It is planned as an urban engine and is intended to stimulate its surroundings through a strong mix of uses. The most unusual aspect of the project was its financing through crowdfunding—5 000 investors made the construction possible and now reap the profits generated by the hotel and by letting. The shared podium with a patio supports two towers. Their stepped profile allows the layout of common green terraces and optimal ventilation and daylighting of the interiors. The building envelope consists of two compositional elements: fair-faced concrete used for the supporting structure and a glass curtain-wall façade. The white grid applied to the glass with ceramic paint varies in intensity. On the one hand, it serves as solar protection, on the other hand, the mass of the building is visually reduced by the vertical structure.

Der Bacatá Tower befindet sich im Herzen Bogotás, nahe dem historischen Zentrum. Er ist als urbaner Motor geplant und soll seine Umgebung durch eine starke Nutzungsmischung stimulieren. Ungewöhnlich an dem Projekt war vor allem die Finanzierung über Crowdfunding – 5000 Investoren machten den Bau möglich und erhalten nun die Gewinne, die mit dem Hotel und durch Vermietungen erzielt werden. Die gemeinsame Sockelzone mit einem Patio trägt zwei Türme. Deren abgetreppte Figur erlaubt grüne Terrassen zur gemeinschaftlichen Nutzung und ermöglicht die optimale Durchlüftung und Belichtung der Innenräume. Die Gebäudehülle besteht aus zwei kompositorischen Elementen: dem Sichtbeton der tragenden Gebäudestruktur und einer vorgehängten Glasfassade. Das weiße, mit Keramikfarbe aufgebrachte Raster auf dem Glas variiert in seiner Intensität. Es dient zum einen als Sonnenschutz, zum anderen wird die Masse des Gebäudes durch die vertikale Gliederung optisch reduziert.

Nominated Project 2020
Nominiertes Projekt 2020

Foster + Partners
COMCAST TECHNOLOGY CENTER
Philadelphia, PA, USA

Architects Architekten **Foster + Partners, London, UK**
Großbritannien
Project architects Projektarchitekten **Norman Foster;**
Kendall Heaton
Architects of record Lokale Architekten
Kendall/Heaton Associates
Client Bauherr **Liberty Property Trust**
Structural engineers Tragwerksplanung **Thornton**
Tomasetti
MEP Haustechnik **BALA Engineers**

Height Höhe **341 m**
Stories Geschosse **60**

Site area Grundstücksfläche **5794 m²**
Building footprint Bebaute Fläche **5794 m²**
Gross floor area Bruttogeschossfläche **123 560 m²**
Structure Konstruktion **Concrete core with steel frame**
Betonkern mit Stahlrahmen
Completion Fertigstellung **Spring** Frühjahr **2019**
Main use Hauptnutzung **Office** Büros

Sustainability:
LEED Platinum certification; active chilled beam
system reduces energy loads and creates a healthier
working environment; triple-height sky gardens
provide daylight

Nachhaltigkeit:
LEED-Zertifizierung in Platin; Deckeninduktions-
durchlass-System reduziert Energielasten und schafft
eine gesündere Arbeitsumgebung; Sky Gardens über
drei Ebenen sorgen für natürliches Licht

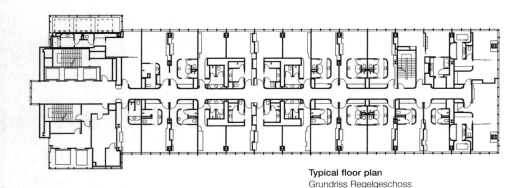

Typical floor plan
Grundriss Regelgeschoss

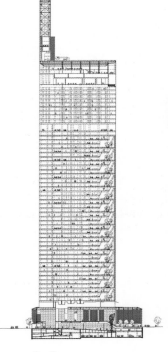

Section
Schnitt

At 341 meters, the Comcast Technology Center is the tallest building in Philadelphia and, with the exception of New York and Chicago, even in the United States. The new high-rise building directly adjacent to the existing Comcast Center is an extension of the cable network operator's corporate headquarters. The two buildings are connected to each other and to the subway by an underground passageway that is alive with shops, artwork and sitting areas. At street level, the building reflects Philadelphia's bourgeois tradition of public spaces: a sheltered 'winter garden' combines elements of a lobby and an urban square to create a flowing transition between interior and exterior, complete with works of art created especially for this area by Jenny Holzer and Conrad Shawcross. On the top twelve stories, the tower accommodates a hotel, a spa, and a restaurant, with a ceiling height extending over three floors, from where an impressive pano-ramic view of the city can be enjoyed.

Mit 341 Metern ist das Comcast Technology Center das höchste Gebäude Philadelphias und, New York und Chicago ausgenommen, sogar der Vereinigten Staaten. Das neue Hochhaus direkt neben dem bestehenden Comcast Center erweitert die Firmenzentrale des Kabelnetzbetreibers. Beide Gebäude sind über eine unterirdische, durch Geschäfte, Kunstwerke und Sitzbereiche belebte Passage sowohl untereinander als auch mit der U-Bahn verbunden. Auf Straßenniveau spiegelt das Gebäude Philadelphias bürgerliche Tradition der öffentlichen Räume wider: Ein geschützter „Wintergarten" kombiniert Elemente einer Lobby und eines urbanen Platzes zu einem fließenden Übergang zwischen innen und außen samt eigens für diesen Bereich geschaffenen Kunstwerken von Jenny Holzer und Conrad Shawcross. In den obersten zwölf Geschossen beherbergt der Turm ein Hotel, ein Spa und ein Restaurant mit einer Deckenhöhe über drei Geschosse, von wo aus sich ein beeindruckender Panoramablick über die Stadt bietet.

Nominated Project 2020
Nominiertes Projekt 2020

Foster + Partners
NATIONAL BANK OF KUWAIT – NBK TOWER
Kuwait City Kuwait-Stadt, **Kuwait**

Architects Architekten **Foster + Partners, London, UK**
Großbritannien
Project architects Projektarchitekten **Stefan Behling,**
Nikolai Malsch, Stuart Latham, Gordon Seiles
Architects of record Lokale Architekten **SSH**
International
Client Bauherr **National Bank of Kuwait**
Structural engineers Tragwerksplanung **Buro Happold**
MEP Haustechnik **Buro Happold**

Height Höhe **300 m**
Stories Geschosse **60**
Site area Grundstücksfläche **6000 m²**
Building footprint Bebaute Fläche **3480 m²**
Gross floor area Bruttogeschossfläche **58 200 m²**
Structure Konstruktion **Composite construction**
Verbundbauweise
Completion Fertigstellung **April 2020**
Main use Hauptnutzung **Office** Büros

Sustainability:
pursuing **LEED Gold** certification; passive and active
measures to reduce water and energy consumption

Nachhaltigkeit:
strebt Leed-Zertifizierung in Gold an; aktive und passive
Maßnahmen zur Senkung des Wasser- und Energie-
verbrauchs

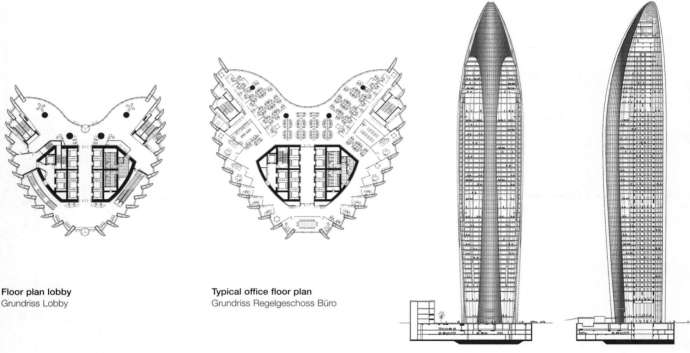

Floor plan lobby
Grundriss Lobby

Typical office floor plan
Grundriss Regelgeschoss Büro

Sections
Schnitte

The unusual shape of the NBK Tower combines structural innovation with a highly efficient façade and protects the offices from the extremes of Kuwait's climate, where summer temperatures average 40 degrees Celsius. The design opens up like a pod towards the north to minimize solar gains, while at the same time affording views of the Arabian Gulf. The south façade is shaded by a series of load-bearing concrete ribs that extend across the full height of the tower. By expanding the volume to approximately three-quarters of the tower's height before tapering off again, the design maximizes the office space on the respective floors, while simultaneously providing shade for the offices below. The crescent-shaped layout allows for both the maximum number of individual offices along the façade and flexible zoning.

Die ungewöhnliche Form des NBK Tower verbindet strukturelle Innovation mit einer hocheffizienten Fassade und schützt die Büros vor den Extremen des Klimas in Kuwait, wo die Temperaturen im Sommer durch-schnittlich 40 Grad betragen. Der Entwurf öffnet sich wie eine Schote nach Norden, um die Sonneneinstrahlung zu minimieren, während er gleichzeitig Blicke auf den Arabischen Golf offenbart. Die Südfassade wird von einer Reihe tragender Betonrippen verschattet, die sich über die volle Höhe des Turms erstrecken. Durch die Ausdehnung des Volumens bis etwa dreiviertel des Turms, bevor er sich wieder verjüngt, maximiert das Design die Büroflächen in den betreffenden Etagen bei gleichzeitiger Verschattung der unteren Büros. Der halbmondförmige Grundriss erlaubt eine größtmögliche Anzahl von Einzelbüros entlang der Fassade, zugleich aber auch flexible Zonierungen.

Nominated Project 2020
Nominiertes Projekt 2020

gmp Architekten von Gerkan, Marg und Partner
POLY GREENLAND PLAZA
Shanghai, China

Architects Architekten **gmp Architekten von Gerkan, Marg und Partner, Hamburg, Germany** Deutschland
Project architects Projektarchitekten **Meinhard von Gerkan; Nikolaus Goetze; Magdalene Weiß**
Architects of record Lokale Architekten **Tongji Architectural Design (Group); Zhongxin Architectural Design & Research Institute**
Client Bauherr **Shanghai Shengguan Real Estate Development**
Structural engineers Tragwerksplanung **Tongji Architectural Design (Group); Zhongxin Architectural Design & Research Institute**
MEP Haustechnik **Tongji Architectural Design (Group); Zhongxin Architectural Design & Research Institute**

Height Höhe **up to** bis **100 m**
Stories Geschosse **up to** bis **23**

Site area Grundstücksfläche **47 478 m²**
Building footprint Bebaute Fläche **16 307 m²**
Gross floor area Bruttogeschossfläche **274 000 m²**
Structure Konstruktion **Reinforced concrete** Stahlbeton
Completion Fertigstellung **June** Juni **2018**
Main use Hauptnutzung **Office and retail** Büros und Einzelhandel

Sustainability:
rainwater harvesting; hot water supply via solar system; sealed surfaces <60 percent; more than 30 percent of the roof areas are greened; walking distance to metro and other local public transport; avoidance of light pollution by glare-free outdoor lights; indoor air quality: CO and CO_2 monitoring

Nachhaltigkeit:
Regenwassernutzung; Warmwasserversorgung über Solaranlage; versiegelte Flächen <60 Prozent; über 30 Prozent der Dachflächen begrünt; fußläufige Anbindung zu Metro und weiteren ÖPNV; Vermeidung von Lichtverschmutzung durch nicht-blendende Außenleuchten; Innenraumluft-qualität: CO und CO_2-Monitoring

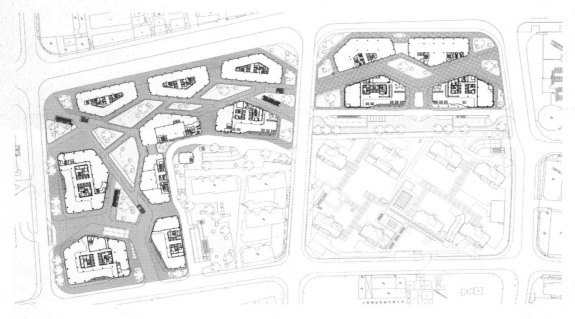

Ground floor plan
Grundriss Erdgeschoss

The complex comprising five towers and seven three- to four-story pavilions creates a coherent quarter in the otherwise heterogeneous Yangpu District. The heights of the individual buildings relate to the surrounding development. To the north, the site adjoins flat industrial complexes, to the south and east it is flanked by residential towers. All buildings have an irregular pentagonal ground plan with rounded corners. The planted green islands on the site take up this design vocabulary. At night, strip lights throughout the entire complex and inside the buildings emphasize the large-scale structures—vertical lighting accentuate the high-rise buildings, horizontal lighting the lower pavilions. At daytime, an irregular white stripe pattern, which contrasts with the dark glass elements, structures the façade of the towers.

Der Komplex aus fünf Hochhäusern und sieben drei- bis vierstöckigen Pavillonbauten bildet ein einheitliches Quartier im ansonsten heterogenen Bezirk Yangpu. Die Höhe der einzelnen Bauten nimmt Bezug auf die umgebende Bebauung. Im Norden grenzt das Areal an flache industrielle Bebauung, im Süden und Osten an Wohnhochhäuser. Alle Baukörper haben eine unregelmäßige Fünfeck-Grundfläche mit abgerundeten Ecken. Diese Formensprache nehmen die bepflanzten Grüninseln auf dem Gelände auf. Bei Nacht akzentuieren Lichtbänder auf dem gesamten Gelände sowie im Inneren der Gebäude die baulichen Großformen – vertikale Bänder die Hochhäuser, horizontale Bänder entsprechend die flachen Bauten. Bei Tag gliedert ein unregelmäßiges weißes Streifenmuster, das sich gegen die dunkle Glasfassade absetzt, die Fassade der Hochhäuser.

GRAFT
LUXE LAKE TOWERS
Chengdu, China

Architects Architekten **GRAFT, Berlin, Germany**
Deutschland
Project architects Projektarchitekten **Lars Krückeberg,**
Wolfram Putz, Thomas Willemeit, Casey McSweeney,
Cesar Alejandro Gonzalez, Chris Li Ju, Dagmar
Niecke, Dorian Bybee, Gregor Hoheisel, John Shen,
Lyla Wu, Yan Gu, Yi Jian
Architects of record Lokale Architekten **China**
Southwest Architectural Design and Research
Institute Co., Ltd.
Client Bauherr **Wide Horizon**
Structural engineers Tragwerksplanung **Chengdu Jing**
Jian Chuan Architectural Engineering Consultant Co.
Ltd.
MEP Haustechnik **Sichuan Guan Jia Construction Co.**
Ltd.

Height Höhe **100 m**
Stories Geschosse **32**
Site area Grundstücksfläche **9600 m²**
Building footprint Bebaute Fläche **1730 m²**
Gross floor area Bruttogeschossfläche **88 100 m²**
Structure Konstruktion **Reinforced concrete**
Stahlbeton
Completion Fertigstellung **November 2019**
Main use Hauptnutzung **Residential** Wohnen

Sustainability:
The project is part of the Luxe Lakes Eco-city in
Chengdu, which has created its own eco-system
around the new buildings; private gardens for the
residents

Nachhaltigkeit:
Das Projekt ist Teil der Ökostadt Luxe Lakes in Chengdu,
die um die Neubauten herum eine eigenes Öko-System
geschaffen hat; private Gärten für die Bewohner

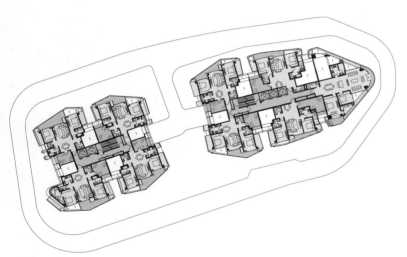

Typical floor plan
Grundriss Regelgeschoss

Section
Schnitt

The Luxe Lake Towers are part of Luxe Lakes Eco-City, a district of Chengdu in the middle of an artificial lake landscape. The design of the towers represents a radical departure from standard residential tower typologies. Nine extremely slender towers, each with a footprint of just one residential unit of 70 to 90 square meters, are grouped into two clusters with a shared circulation core. Each apartment has a small private garden measuring eight square meters. The position of the gardens alternates from floor to floor, enabling their two-story height. The façades are defined by the shell structure of the nine towers and the balcony balustrades made of highly reflective glass. Sculpturally shaped pilotis allow the landscape on the ground floor to flow beneath the towers, creating a pleasant natural breeze in the subtropical monsoon climate of Sichuan.

Die Luxe Lake Towers sind Teil der Luxe Lakes Eco-City, ein Stadtteil Chengdus inmitten einer künstlichen Seenlandschaft. Das Design der Türme bietet eine radikale Abkehr von Standard-Wohnturmtypologien. Neun extrem schlanke Türme, deren Grundfläche von jeweils nur einer 70 bis 90 Quadratmeter großen Wohneinheit eingenommen wird, sind zu zwei Clustern mit einem gemeinsamen Erschließungskern gebündelt. Jedes Apartment verfügt über einen kleinen privaten Garten von acht Quadratmetern. Die Position der Gärten alternieren von Stockwerk zu Stockwerk, was deren zweigeschossige Höhe ermöglicht. Die Fassaden werden durch die Schalenstruktur der neun Türme sowie die Balkonbalustrade aus hochreflektierendem Glas definiert. Skulptural ausgeformte Pilotis lassen die Landschaft im Erdgeschoss unter den Türmen hindurchfließen, und es entsteht eine natürliche Brise, die im subtropischen Monsunklima von Sichuan angenehm ist.

Nominated Project 2020
Nominiertes Projekt 2020

Kohn Pedersen Fox Associates
CHINA RESOURCES TOWER
Shenzhen, China

Architects Architekten **Kohn Pedersen Fox Associates, New York, NY, USA**
Project architects Projektarchitekten **James von Klemperer; Inkai Mu; Bernard Chang; Brian Chung; Jorge Mendoza; Alkis Klimathianos; Joyce Lam**
Architects of record Lokale Architekten **CCDI Group**
Client Bauherr **Constructa China Resources**
Structural engineers Tragwerksplanung **Arup; CCDI Group**
MEP Haustechnik **WSP Group; CCDI Group**

Height Höhe **392.5 m**
Stories Geschosse **67**
Site area Grundstücksfläche **15 718 m²**
Building footprint Bebaute Fläche **3018 m²**
Gross floor area Bruttogeschossfläche **108 875 m²**

Structure Konstruktion **Reinforced concrete** Stahlbeton
Completion Fertigstellung **December** Dezember **2018**
Main use Hauptnutzung **Office** Büros

Sustainability:
the building's overall performance and efficiency-supporting shape; cylindrical shape reduces the solar exposure of the façade as the glass panels are faceted away from the sunlight; deep fins that collapse away from the direction of the sun additionally create a shading barrier; high performance façade; exo-structural system reduces wind loads and ensures efficient construction by using less building materials

Nachhaltigkeit:
Gesamtleistung sowie Form des Gebäudes, die dessen Wirtschaftlichkeit unterstützt; zylindrische Form reduziert die Sonneneinstrahlung auf die Fassade, da die Glaspaneele von der Sonneneinstrahlung abgewandt sind; tiefe Lamellen, die gegen die Sonnenrichtung wegklappen, bilden zusätzlich eine Verschattungsbarriere; Hochleistungsfassade; das außenliegende Tragsystem reduziert die Windlasten und gewährleistet durch den geringeren Einsatz von Baumaterialien eine effiziente Errichtung

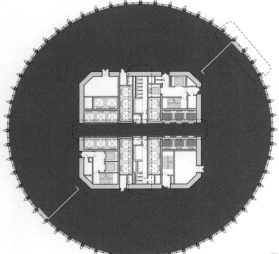
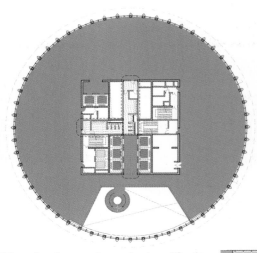

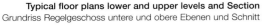
Typical floor plans lower and upper levels and Section
Grundriss Regelgeschoss untere und obere Ebenen und Schnitt

The China Resources Tower is located on the shore of the Bay of Shenzhen in the Houhai Business District between a sports complex in the north and a park in the south. The façade structure of what is currently the third tallest building in the city consists of a diamond-shaped *exoskeleton*, which allows column-free office floors inside. At the top of the conically tapering tower, these external supports converge into a single point. Below this is an impressive *Sky Hall*. Looking upwards at the complicated geometric pattern, it is reminiscent of a Gothic rose window, creating an almost sacred spatial effect. At the base, the canopies of the entrances develop dynamically from the diamond-shaped façade structure. The interplay of geometric shapes continues inside, for example on the folded ceiling in the foyer.

Der China Resources Tower ist am Ufer der Bucht von Shenzhen im Houhai Business District zwischen einem Sportkomplex im Norden und einem Park im Süden platziert. Die Fassadenstruktur des aktuell dritthöchsten Gebäudes der Stadt besteht aus einem rautenförmigen „Exoskelett", das im Inneren stützenfreie Büroetagen ermöglicht. An der Spitze des sich konisch verjüngenden Turms laufen diese außenliegenden Stützen zu einem einzigen Punkt zusammen. Darunter befindet sich eine beeindruckende „Sky Hall". Blickt man nach oben auf das komplizierte geometrische Muster, erinnert dies an ein gotisches Rosenfenster, wodurch eine fast sakrale Raumwirkung entsteht. An der Basis entwickeln sich die Vordächer der Eingänge dynamisch aus der Rautenstruktur der Fassade. Auch im Inneren setzt sich das Spiel mit geometrischen Formen fort, so zum Beispiel an der gefalteten Decke des Foyers.

Nominated Project 2020
Nominiertes Projekt 2020

Kohn Pedersen Fox Associates
MGM COTAI
Macau, China

Architects Architekten **Kohn Pedersen Fox Associates, London, UK** Großbritannien
Project architects Projektarchitekten **John Bushell; Shawn Duffy; Maciej Olczyk; Ko Makabe; Hide Furuta; Rob Starsmore**
Architects of record Lokale Architekten **Eddie Wong & Associates; Wong & Tung International**
Client Bauherr **MGM Resorts International**
Structural engineers Tragwerksplanung **Arup; Siu Yin Wai**
MEP Haustechnik **JBA Consulting Engineers**

Height Höhe **151 m**
Stories Geschosse **35**
Site area Grundstücksfläche **71 833 m²**
Gross floor area Bruttogeschossfläche **287 322 m²**
Structure Konstruktion **Reinforced concrete** Stahlbeton

Completion Fertigstellung **February** Februar **2018**
Main use Hauptnutzung **Mixed use comprising casino, hotel, retail, gastronomy** Mischnutzung aus Casino, Hotel, Einzelhandel und Gastronomie

Sustainability:
500 m² green wall with innovative and resource-efficient watering system; advanced and efficient electricity, water and natural gas supply systems; external energy recovery and reuse system for cooling air and water in the resort; building management system capable, for example, of automatically adjusting the air conditioning system to changes in the weather

Nachhaltigkeit:
500 m² große begrünte Wand mit innovativem und ressourceneffizientem Bewässerungssystem; moderne und effiziente Strom-, Wasser- und Erdgasversorgungs-systeme; externes Energierückgewinnungs- und -wieder-verwendungssystem für die Kühlung von Luft und Wasser im Resort; Gebäudemanagementsystem, das z.B. die Klimaanlage automatisch an Wetteränderungen anpassen kann

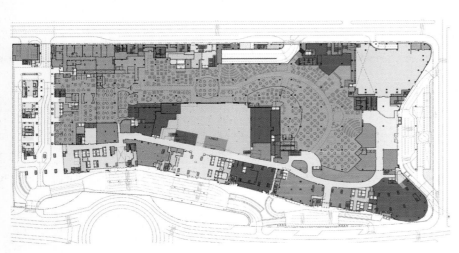

Site plan
Lageplan

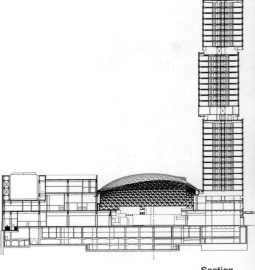

Section
Schnitt

The MGM Cotai Casino and Resort consists of nine boxes, apparently stacked on top of each other, whose glass façades are colored differently and glisten in silver, gold and bronze. By dividing the building mass into rectangular cubes, they can follow the curved western site boundary. The 38 floors accommodate the hotel with 1,600 rooms, suites, private gambling rooms and a spa. The cubes are positioned on a two-story podium that fills the entire block. In the center of the podium, directly adjoining the hotel lobby is the *Spectacle Space*, which is spanned by the world's largest self-supporting lattice shell. An entrance on the north side of the block leads visitors directly to the actual casino area including a theatre, retail areas and restaurants.

Das Casino und Resort MGM Cotai besteht aus neun scheinbar aufeinandergestapelten Boxen, deren Glas-fassaden unterschiedlich eingefärbt sind und silbern, golden und bronzen funkeln. Durch die Aufteilung der Baumasse in rechtwinklige Kuben können diese der Krümmung der westlichen Grundstücksgrenze folgen. In den insgesamt 38 Stockwerken befindet sich das Hotel mit 1600 Zimmern, Suiten, privaten Spielzimmern und einem Spa. Die Kuben stehen auf einem zweistöckigen Sockel, der den gesamten Block ausfüllt. Im Zentrum des Sockels schließt sich direkt an die Hotellobby der „Spectacle Space" an, der von der weltgrößten frei-tragenden Gitterschale überspannt wird. Ein Eingang an der Nordseite des Blocks führt die Besucher direkt zum eigentlichen Casinobereich samt Theater, Einzelhandels-flächen und Restaurants.

Nominated Project 2020
Nominiertes Projekt 2020

Kohn Pedersen Fox Associates
ROBINSON TOWER
Singapore Singapur

Architects Architekten **Kohn Pedersen Fox**
Associates, New York, NY, USA
Project architect Projektarchitekt **Robert Whitlock**
Architects of record Lokale Architekten **A61**
Client Bauherr **Tuan Sing Holdings**
Structural engineers Tragwerksplanung **KTP**
Consultants
MEP Haustechnik **TY Lin International Group**

Height Höhe **180 m**
Stories Geschosse **28**
Site area Grundstücksfläche **1725 m²**
Building footprint Bebaute Fläche **933 m²**
Gross floor area Bruttogeschossfläche **18 014 m²**
Structure Konstruktion **Reinforced concrete**
Stahlbeton
Completion Fertigstellung **September 2018**
Main use Hauptnutzung **Office, retail, public gardens**
Büros, Einzelhandel, öffentliche Gärten

Sustainability:
BCA Green Mark Platinum; open floor plans with
an offset core to the west limit solar heat gain;
seamless circulation system facilitates movement
throughout the podium and culminates at the rooftop
gardens; terraced gardens provide a variety of
important environmental benefits and also address
the newly developed Land Replacement Area
requirements, an response to land lost due to
development; elevated gardens increase light and air
at ground level, increase water efficiency and
decrease heat gain

Nachhaltigkeit:
BCA Green Mark in Platin; offene Grundrisse mit einem
nach Westen versetzten Kern begrenzen den solaren
Wärmeeintrag; nahtloses Erschließungssystem verein-
facht die Bewegung im gesamten Sockelbereich
und endet in den Dachgärten; Terrassengärten bieten
eine Vielzahl wichtiger Umweltvorteile und reagieren auf
die neu entwickelten Flächenanforderungen für Land-
ersatz, eine Antwort auf den Verlust von Land durch
Bebauung; hoch gelegene Gärten ermöglichen eben-
erdig mehr Licht und Luft, erhöhen die Wassereffizienz
und verringern den Wärmeeintrag

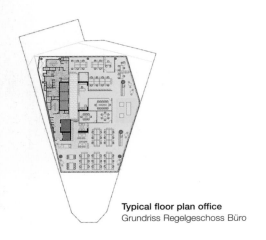

Typical floor plan office
Grundriss Regelgeschoss Büro

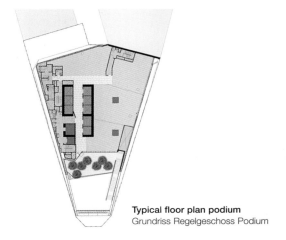

Typical floor plan podium
Grundriss Regelgeschoss Podium

Situated on a wedge-shaped site between two
streets, Robinson Tower is precisely integrated into
the urban situation. The podium makes almost
complete use of the site area, but leaves enough
space at the tip to create a small public square in
front. Supported only by the circulation core and two
additional columns, the office tower almost seems to
float above the stepped terraces of the seven-story
podium. At the same time, the division into two
volumes creates a human scale. Refractions of light
on the facetted glass façade transform the building
into a sparkling crystal. The crystalline form reduces
direct views into and out of adjacent high-rise
buildings and allows natural light to enter even the
lower stories. At the top of the tower is a sky garden.

Auf einem keilförmigen Grundstück zwischen zwei
Straßen gelegen, ist der Robinson Tower präzise in die
städtebauliche Situation eingebunden. Der Sockelbau
nutzt das Grundstück nahezu ganz aus, lässt jedoch
genug Raum, dass an der Spitze davor ein kleiner
öffentlicher Platz entsteht. Getragen nur vom
Erschließungskern und zwei weiteren Stützen, scheint
der Büroturm fast über den abgetreppten Terrassen des
siebengeschossigen Sockels zu schweben. Gleichzeitig
schafft die Unterteilung in zwei Volumen einen
menschlichen Maßstab. Brechungen des Lichts auf der
facettierten Glasfassade machen aus dem Bau einen
funkelnden Kristall. Die kristalline Form vermindert direkte
Einblicke in und aus angrenzenden Hochhäusern und
ermöglicht den Einfall natürlichen Lichts auch in untere
Stockwerke. An der Spitze des Turms befindet sich ein
Sky Garden.

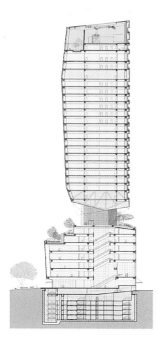

Section
Schnitt

LEGORRETA
MIYANA, TORRE CHAPULÍN
Mexico City Mexiko-Stadt, **Mexico** Mexiko

Architects Architekten **LEGORRETA, Mexico City**
Mexiko-Stadt, **Mexico** Mexiko
Project architects Projektarchitekten Ricardo
Legorreta, Víctor Legorreta, Miguel Almaraz, Adriana
Ciklik, Carlos Vargas, Miguel Alatriste, Emmanuel
Pérez, Fernando López, Oscar Islas, Luis Oviedo,
Johanna Miñarro, Giovanna Arce
Architects of record Lokale Architekten **Grupo
Architech**
Client Bauherr **Gigante Grupo Inmobiliario**
Structural engineers Tragwerksplanung **Colinas de
Buen; VSL-DOCSA; Postensa**
MEP Haustechnik **DYPRO; FLG; Cien Acres**

Height Höhe **172 m**
Stories Geschosse **44**
Site area Grundstücksfläche **3935 m²**
Building footprint Bebaute Fläche **2464 m²**
Gross floor area Bruttogeschossfläche **53 574 m²**
Structure Konstruktion **Concrete and steel**
Beton und Stahl
Completion Fertigstellung **April 2020**
Main use Hauptnutzung **Residential** Wohnen

Sustainability:
Minimum requirements stipulated in construction codes were surpassed by nearly three times; aims to achieve the LEED for Neighborhood Development certification—this includes a certain amount of green areas, water reuse, and LED lighting system with motion sensors; endemic vegetation, thus less water consumption; all construction materials were found within a maximum radius of 80 km from the site; use of recycled construction materials, e.g. for all of the built-in furniture and wooden carpentry elements; windows were treated differently according to orientation and respond to solar radiation; natural cross-ventilation; parking areas are naturally ventilated

Nachhaltigkeit:
Die in den Bauvorschriften festgelegten Mindestanforderungen wurden um nahezu das Dreifache übertroffen; angestrebt wird die Zertifizierung LEED for Neighborhood Development – dies beinhaltet eine gewisse Anzahl von Grünflächen, Wasserwiederverwendung und ein LED-Beleuchtungssystem mit Bewegungsmeldern; endemische Pflanzenarten, daher weniger Wasserverbrauch; alle Baumaterialien stammen aus einem Umkreis von maximal 80 km um das Grundstück; Verwendung von recycelten Baumaterialien, z.B. für sämtliche Einbaumöbel und Tischlerelemente aus Holz; Fenster wurden je nach Ausrichtung und Sonneneinstrahlung unterschiedlich behandelt; natürliche Querbelüftung; Parkplätze werden natürlich belüftet

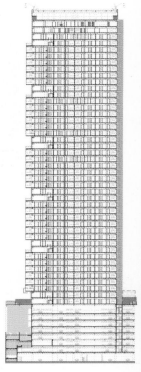

Section
Schnitt

Typical floor plan
Grundriss Regelgeschoss

The Miyana mixed-use complex consists of three residential and two office towers, one of which is still under construction, standing on a common multi-story podium. This podium, which accommodates retail shops, restaurants and a car park, links the complex to the public space and the surrounding area. At a height of 20 meters, it provides communal facilities reserved for the residents of the complex, including a pool, a football pitch, a fitness studio and a café along with a green area of 10 000 square meters. Visually, residential and office towers can be clearly distinguished from one another. While the residential towers have a beige-colored punctuated façade with windows in various formats put over it like a slipcase, leaving the narrow sides free, the completed office tower has a light-colored façade with regular ribbon windows.

Der Mixed-Use-Komplex Miyana besteht aus drei Wohn- und zwei Bürohochhäusern, davon eines noch im Bau, die auf einem gemeinsamen mehrstöckigen Sockel stehen. Der Sockel, in dem Einzelhandel, Restaurants und Parken untergebracht sind, verknüpft den Komplex mit dem öffentlichen Raum und der Umgebung. Auf ihm, in 20 Metern Höhe, befinden sich Gemeinschaftseinrichtungen, die den Bewohnern des Komplexes vorbehalten sind – neben einer Grünfläche von 10 000 Quadratmetern unter anderem ein Pool, ein Fußballfeld, ein Fitnessstudio und ein Café. Optisch sind Wohn- und Bürohochhäuser klar voneinander zu unterscheiden. Während den Wohntürmen eine beigefarbene Lochfassade mit Fenstern in unterschiedlichen Formaten schuberartig übergestülpt ist und die Schmalseiten frei bleiben, zeigt der fertiggestellte Büroturm eine helle Fassade mit regelmäßigen Fensterbändern.

Nominated Project 2020
Nominiertes Projekt 2020

Magnus Kaminiarz & Cie. Architektur
GRAND TOWER
Frankfurt am Main, Germany Deutschland

Architects Architekten **Magnus Kaminiarz & Cie.**
Architektur, Frankfurt am Main, Germany Deutschland
Client Bauherr **gsp Städtebau**
Structural engineers Tragwerksplanung **AWD**
Ingenieurgemeinschaft, EHS beratende Ingenieure
für Bauwesen
MEP Haustechnik **Ventury, pbe-Beljuli**

Height Höhe **180 m**
Stories Geschosse **48**
Site area Grundstücksfläche **3222 m²**
Building footprint Bebaute Fläche **1011 m²**
Gross floor area Bruttogeschossfläche **44 000 m²**
Structure Konstruktion **Reinforced concrete**
Stahlbeton
Completion Fertigstellung **April 2020**
Main use Hauptnutzung **Residential** Wohnen

Sustainability:
heating via district heating; heat exchangers reduce
energy loss through exhaust air; smart lift control
system; thermal insulation glazing reduces heat loss;
shape reduces heat input; extensive garbage
separation plan

Nachhaltigkeit:
Heizung über Fernwärme; Wärmetauscher reduzieren
Energieverlust durch Abluft; intelligentes Aufzugs-
steuerungssystem; Wärmeschutzverglasung reduziert
Wärmeverlust; Gebäudeform reduziert Wärmeeintrag;
weitreichender Mülltrennungsplan

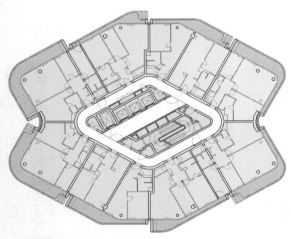

Typical floor plan
Grundriss Regelgeschoss

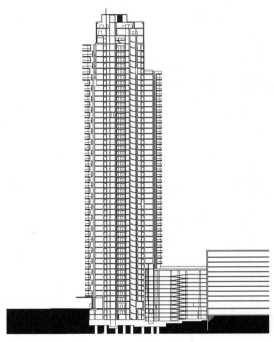

Section
Schnitt

Its expressive design and curved balcony elements
make Germany's tallest residential high-rise building
a new landmark in Frankfurt's Europaviertel. The
balconies provide optimum sun protection to reduce
solar gain, reduce the wind loads acting on the
building, and ensure a high level of privacy for the
residents. The respective orientation of the
apartments is based on the course of the sun and
the available views. Flexible floor plans, high
ceilings, and panoramic windows offer bright and
open apartments, which, due to their variety of
types, allow efficient use of space. The slender
shape of the high-rise building is made possible by a
core with peripheral anchorage in the circulation
corridor walls and by load-bearing partition walls.

Mit seiner expressiven Gestaltung und den
geschwungenen Balkonelementen wird das höchste
Wohnhochhaus Deutschlands zum neuen Landmark in
Frankfurts Europaviertel. Die Balkone bilden einen
optimalen Sonnenschutz zur Reduzierung des Hitze-
eintrags, sie vermindern die Windlasten, die auf das
Gebäude wirken, und sorgen für ein hohes Maß an
Privatsphäre für die Bewohner. Die jeweilige Ausrichtung
der Wohnungen orientiert sich am Lauf der Sonne und
an den Aussichten, die sich bieten. Freie Grundrisse,
hohe Decken und Panoramafenster bieten helle und
offene Wohnungen, die durch ihren Typenreichtum eine
gute Flächenausnutzung ermöglichen. Die schmale Figur
des Hochhauses wird durch einen Kern mit Ringanker in
den Erschließungsgangwänden und durch tragende
Trennwände erreicht.

Morphosis Architects
CASABLANCA FINANCE CITY TOWER
Casablanca, Morocco Marokko

Architects Architekten **Morphosis Architects, Culver City, CA, USA**
Project architects Projektarchitekten **Thom Mayne; Ung-Joo Scott Lee; Nicolas Fayad; Stuart Franks; Hunter Knight**
Architects of record Lokale Architekten **Omar Alaoui Architectes**
Client Bauherr **Casablanca Finance City**
Structural engineers Tragwerksplanung **Thornton Tomasetti; Arup**
MEP Haustechnik **Tractebel Engineering**

Height Höhe **121 m**
Stories Geschosse **25**
Site area Grundstücksfläche **1502 m²**
Building footprint Bebaute Fläche **669 m²**
Gross floor area Bruttogeschossfläche **19 845 m²**
Structure Konstruktion **Reinforced concrete and steel** Stahlbeton und Stahl
Completion Fertigstellung **April 2019**
Main use Hauptnutzung **Office** Büros

Sustainability:
LEED Gold certification; brise-soleil system protecting against the sun, while still allowing the building to use external elements to regulate natural light, air, and temperatures internally; additional features include tenant submetering for lighting, plug loads, heating, cooling, and water, as well as the use of occupancy sensors for lighting control

Nachhaltigkeit:
LEED-Zertifizierung in Gold; Brise-Soleil-System zum Schutz vor Sonneneinstrahlung, wobei das Gebäude auch externe Elemente zur Regulierung von natürlichem Licht, Luft und Temperatur im Inneren nutzen kann; zusätzliche Merkmale umfassen das Submetering der Mieter für Licht, Strom, Heizung, Kühlung und Wasser sowie den Einsatz von Präsenzmeldern zur Beleuchtungssteuerung

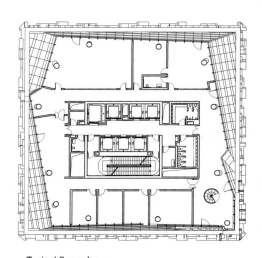

Typical floor plan
Grundriss Regelgeschoss

Section
Schnitt

The tower is the prelude to the new Casablanca Finance City (CFC) in Morocco, the traditional gateway to Africa. As a hub between the African continent and the rest of the world, the planned economic and financial center is intended to encourage international investors and companies to locate their headquarters here and invest in Africa. The CFC Tower stands in the shimmering heat of the Moroccan desert like a cool white iceberg. The office tower clearly rises above its surroundings and presents different perspectives from all directions. A brise-soleil system that seems to wrapped around the tower protects the offices from the glaring sun but at the same time allows views of the city. The jagged crown with its refractions and folds is mirrored at the base, creating exciting connections to the public space.

Das Hochhaus bildet den Auftakt für die neue Casablanca Finance City (CFC) in Marokko, dem traditionellen Einfallstor nach Afrika. Als Drehscheibe zwischen dem afrikanischen Kontinent und dem Rest der Welt soll das geplante Wirtschafts- und Finanzzentrum internationale Investoren und Firmen dazu anregen, hier ihre Geschäftssitze anzusiedeln und in Afrika zu investieren. Wie ein kühler weißer Eisberg steht der CFC Tower in der flirrenden Hitze der Wüste Marokkos. Der Büroturm ragt deutlich aus seiner Umgebung heraus und bietet aus allen Richtungen unterschiedliche Ansichten. Scheinbar um den Turm gewickelte Brise Soleils schützen die Büros vor der gleißenden Sonne, lassen aber gleichzeitig Ausblicke in die Stadt zu. Die gezackte Krone mit Ihren Brechungen und Faltungen ist an der Basis gespiegelt, wodurch spannungsreiche Beziehungen zum öffentlichen Raum entstehen.

Nominated Project 2020
Nominiertes Projekt 2020

Rafael Viñoly Architects
NEMA CHICAGO
Chicago, IL, USA

Architects Architekten **Rafael Viñoly Architects**, New York, NY, USA
Project architects Projektarchitekten **Chan-Li Lin; Jay Bargman**
Client Bauherr **Crescent Heights**
Structural engineers Tragwerksplanung **Magnusson Klemencic Associates**
MEP Haustechnik **Thomas A. Gilbertson & Associates**

Height Höhe **273 m**
Stories Geschosse **76**
Site area Grundstücksfläche **3647 m²**
Building footprint Bebaute Fläche **3276 m²**
Gross floor area Bruttogeschossfläche **66 670 m²**
Structure Konstruktion **Steel** Stahl
Completion Fertigstellung **November 2019**
Main use Hauptnutzung **Residential** Wohnen

Sustainability:
LEED Silver certification (aspired); walk score of 91, transit score of 100, situated to minimize reliance on automobiles; energy-saving features; smart building technology based on outdoor environmental conditions; energy-saving residential appliances; LED lighting fixtures; individual programmable thermostats; storm water collection system; green roofs; recycled-content building materials minimize urban heat island effect and maximize interior air quality

Nachhaltigkeit:
LEED-Zertifizierung in Silber (angestrebt); Walk Score von 91, Transit Score von 100, so gelegen, dass die Abhängigkeit vom Auto minimiert wird; Energiespar-funktionen; intelligente Gebäudetechnologie basierend auf äußeren Umweltbedingungen; energiesparende Wohnungsausstattung; LED-Beleuchtungskörper; individuell programmierbare Thermostate; Regenwasser-auffangsystem; begrünte Dächer; Baumaterialien mit Recyclinganteil minimieren den Hitzeinsel-Effekt in der Stadt und maximieren die Luftqualität in Innenräumen

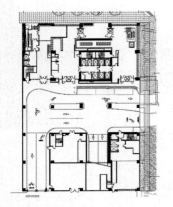

Ground floor plan
Grundriss Erdgeschoss

Floor plan level 18 / 57
Grundriss 18./ 57. Obergeschoss

Section
Schnitt

NEMA Chicago is the tallest purely residential high-rise in the city. It is located on the southwest corner of Grant Park, in the heart of the rapidly developing South Loop neighborhood. The reduced, stepped building shape is inspired by iconic buildings on Chicago's skyline. The structural module, a nine-square grid, allows great planning flexibility within the 800 column-free rental units. Thanks to bracing building services stories, the tower can also do without large load-bearing walls. A damping system in the upper part of the tower absorbs lateral vibrations. The fair-faced concrete shell of the tower was protected against freeze-thaw cycles with plastic-coated reinforcement and a special cement mix.

NEMA Chicago ist das höchste reine Wohnhochhaus der Stadt. Es liegt an der südwestlichen Ecke des Grant Park, im Herzen des sich schnell entwickelnden Viertels South Loop. Die reduzierte, abgestufte Gebäudeform orientiert sich an ikonischen Bauten der Skyline Chicagos. Das strukturelle Modul, ein Neun-Quadrat-Raster, bietet große Planungsflexibilität innerhalb der 800 stützenfreien Wohneinheiten. Durch aussteifende Technikgeschosse kommt das Gebäude zudem ohne große Wandscheiben aus. Ein Dämpfungssystem im oberen Teil des Turms fängt seitliche Schwingungen ab. Die Sichtbetonhülle des Gebäudes wurde durch eine mit Kunststoff beschichtete Bewehrung und einen speziellen Zementmix gegen Frost-Tau-Wechsel geschützt.

Nominated Project 2020
Nominiertes Projekt 2020

Richard Meier & Partners Architects
TORRES CUARZO
Mexico City Mexiko-Stadt, **Mexico** Mexiko

Architects Architekten **Richard Meier & Partners
Architects, New York, NY, USA**
Project architects Projektarchitekten **Bernhard Karpf;
Rinko Offermann; David Davila**
Architects of record Lokale Architekten **Diametro
Arquitectos**
Client Bauherr **Diametro Arquitectos**
Structural engineers Tragwerksplanung **WSP Group**
MEP Haustechnik **DYPRO; Garza Maldonado y
Asociados; COESA**

Height Höhe **180 m; 100 m**
Stories Geschosse **40; 27**
Site area Grundstücksfläche **4715 m²**
Building footprint Bebaute Fläche **4000 m²**

Gross floor area Bruttogeschossfläche **120 155 m²**
Structure Konstruktion **Concrete and steel** Beton und
Stahl
Completion Fertigstellung **May** Mai **2019**
Main use Hauptnutzung **Mixed use comprising office,
hotel, retail, restaurants** Mischnutzung aus Büros,
Hotel, Einzelhandel und Restaurants

Sustainability:
**The openness of lobbies, stairs, terraces, corridors
and strategically placed operable windows
allow natural light to enter and air to flow through
the voids, minimizing mechanical ventilation
requirements**

Nachhaltigkeit:
Die offene Gestaltung von Lobbys, Treppen, Terrassen
und Korridoren sowie strategisch platzierte, zu öffnende
Fenster lassen Tageslicht einfallen und Luft durch die
Lufträume strömen, sodass Anforderungen an die
mechanische Belüftung minimiert werden

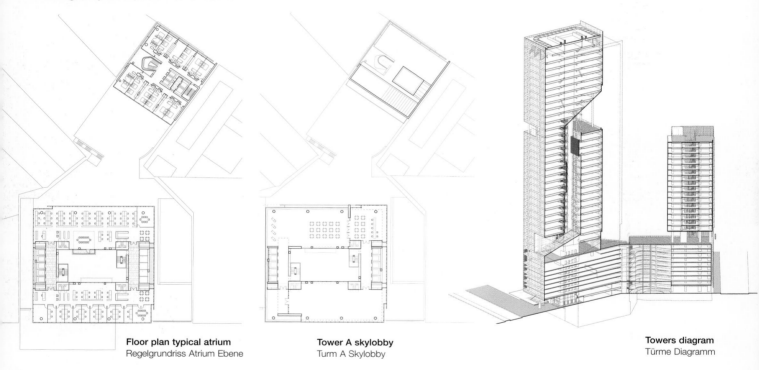

Floor plan typical atrium
Regelgrundriss Atrium Ebene

Tower A skylobby
Turm A Skylobby

Towers diagram
Türme Diagramm

Torres Cuarzo is located at an important crossroads
in Mexico City, between Paseo de la Reforma, a
main shopping boulevard, and El Zocalo, the historic
center. The ensemble, consisting of two towers
connected by a podium, accommodates a variety of
uses. A public space, the Zocalito, permeates the
complex as an elevated square and lobby. It
connects the two towers with each other and the
new development with the city. This makes the
podium an intersection of the different functions. A
central void cut into the volume of the taller of the
two towers creates unconventional but naturally lit
and ventilated floor plans that contribute to a
pleasant working climate.

Die Torres Cuarzo liegen an einer bedeutenden
Kreuzung in Mexiko-Stadt, zwischen dem Paseo de la
Reforma, einem Haupteinkaufsboulevard, und El Zocalo,
dem historischen Zentrum. Das Ensemble, bestehend
aus zwei durch einen Sockelbau verbundenen Türmen,
umfasst eine Vielzahl von Nutzungen. Ein öffentlicher
Raum, der Zocal-ito, durchzieht den Komplex als
angehobener Platz und als Lobby. Er verbindet sowohl
die beiden Türme miteinander als auch das Gebäude
mit der Stadt. Dadurch wird der Sockel zu einem
Knotenpunkt der unterschiedlichen Funktionen. Durch
einen zentralen, in das Volumen des höheren der beiden
Türme geschnittenen Luftraum entstehen unkonven-
tionelle, aber natürlich belichtete und belüftete Grundrisse, die zu einem angenehmen Arbeitsklima
beitragen.

Nominated Project 2020
Nominiertes Projekt 2020

Rogers Stirk Harbour & Partners
3 WORLD TRADE CENTER
New York, NY, USA

Architects Architekten **Rogers Stirk Harbour &
Partners, London, UK** Großbritannien
Project architect Projektarchitekt **Richard Paul**
Architects of record Lokale Architekten **Adamson
Associates**
Client Bauherr **Silverstein Properties Inc.**
Structural engineers Tragwerksplanung **WSP Cantor
Seinuk**
MEP Haustechnik **Jaros, Baum & Bolles**

Height Höhe **330 m**
Stories Geschosse **80**
Site area Grundstücksfläche **5574 m²**
Building footprint Bebaute Fläche **4961 m²**

Gross floor area Bruttogeschossfläche **260 129 m²**
Structure Konstruktion **Steel and concrete**
Stahl und Beton
Completion Fertigstellung **June** Juni **2018**
Main use Hauptnutzung **Office** Büros

Sustainability:
**LEED Gold certification; full-height glazing
maximizes daylight supply; all occupied spaces are
supplied with more filtered outside air than required;
this air is filtered using fine particulate and activated
carbon filters with an efficiency of 95 percent**

Nachhaltigkeit:
LEED-Zertifizierung in Gold; geschosshohe Verglasung
maximiert die Tageslichtversorgung; alle bewohnten
Räume werden mit mehr gefilterter Außenluft versorgt
als vorgeschrieben; die Luft wird mit Feinstaub- und
Aktivkohlefiltern mit einer Effizienz von 95 Prozent
gefiltert

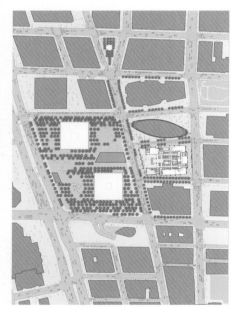

Site plan
Lageplan

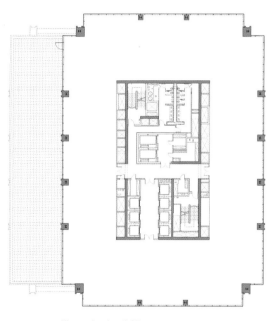

Floor plan level 62
Grundriss 62. Obergeschoss

The second largest building on the World Trade
Center site is another important part of the master
plan for the area, completed 17 years after the
attacks. Located between 1WTC and 4WTC next to
the still empty building site for 2WTC, the new tower
blends into the development surrounding the World
Trade Center Memorial, not least because of the
materiality of the blue glass façade. The main tower
takes up the width of the square between the
memorial's water basins and visually extends it in a
vertical direction, while the two lateral volumes are
aligned with the height of the neighboring buildings.
Beneath the public podium, underground shopping
arcades on several levels connect 3WTC with the
other towers of the complex and directly with the
WTC Transportation Hub by Santiago Calatrava.

Mit dem zweitgrößten Gebäude des World-Trade-Center-
Areals wurde 17 Jahre nach den Anschlägen ein weiterer
wichtiger Bestandteil des Masterplans für das Gelände
fertiggestellt. Zwischen dem 1WTC und dem 4WTC
neben dem noch leeren Bauplatz für das 2WTC fügt sich
der neue Turm nicht zuletzt durch die Materialität der
blauen Glasfassade in die Bebauung ein, die das World
Trade Center Memorial umgibt. Dabei nimmt der Haupt-
baukörper die Breite des Platzes zwischen den Wasser-
becken der Gedenkstätte auf und verlängert sie optisch
in die Vertikale, während sich die beiden seitlichen
Baukörper an den Höhen der umliegenden Gebäude
orientieren. Unter dem öffentlichen Podium ist das 3WTC
unterirdisch über Einkaufspassagen auf mehreren
Ebenen mit den anderen Türmen des Komplexes
verbunden sowie direkt an den WTC Transportation Hub
von Santiago Calatrava angeschlossen.

Section
Schnitt

Nominated Project 2020
Nominiertes Projekt 2020

Safdie Architects
GOLDEN DREAM BAY
Qinhuangdao, China

Architects Architekten **Safdie Architects, Somerville, MA, USA**
Project architect Projektarchitekt **Moshe Safdie**
Architects of record Lokale Architekten **Shanghai Architectural Design and Research Institute (SADRI)**
Client Bauherr **Kerry Properties Ltd.**
Structural engineers Tragwerksplanung **Shanghai Architectural Design and Research Institute (SADRI)**

Height Höhe **100 m**
Stories Geschosse **30**
Site area Grundstücksfläche **59 171 m²**
Building footprint Bebaute Fläche **7900 m²**
Gross floor area Bruttogeschossfläche **152 433 m²**
Structure Konstruktion **Reinforced concrete and steel** Stahlbeton und Stahl
Completion Fertigstellung **January** Januar **2017**
Main use Hauptnutzung **Residential** Wohnen

Sustainability:
Terraces provide the opportunity for staying outdoors in good weather, thus minimizing the need for air-conditioning; balconies and projecting bays provide shading for units below; slender depth of the blocks allows for mostly through units, thus maximizing cross ventilation; in-floor radiant tubes provide efficient heating in winter; extensive planted roofs help retain rainwater, control runoff, reduce temperature swings, and reduce the heat island effect

Nachhaltigkeit:
Terrassen bieten die Möglichkeit, sich bei gutem Wetter im Freien aufzuhalten, wodurch der Klimatisierungs-bedarf minimiert wird; Balkone und vorspringende Erker verschatten die darunterliegenden Wohneinheiten; die geringe Tiefe der Blöcke ermöglicht mehrheitlich durchgehende Wohnungen, wodurch die Querlüftung maximiert wird; Strahlrohre im Boden gewährleisten effizientes Heizen im Winter; großflächige begrünte Dächer tragen dazu bei, Regenwasser zurückzuhalten, den Wasserabfluss zu kontrollieren, Temperatur-schwankungen zu mildern und den Wärmeinseleffekt zu verringern

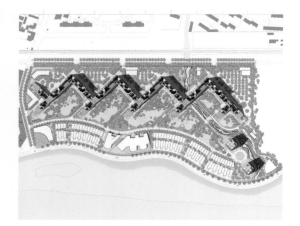

Site plan
Lageplan

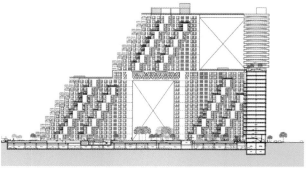

Section
Schnitt

With this project, located 200 kilometers east of Beijing, Moshe Safdie is now transforming his design idea of Habitat 67 in Montreal into a much larger scale. The first two of four planned, high-density blocks are lined up at a 90-degree angle in a specially laid out park. Between the offset stacked volumes there are large openings lined with shops. In addition to providing a wide range of shopping facilities, they create a connection to the adjacent beach promenade. The communal terraces connecting the buildings and the stepped private balconies offer a direct view of the sea. Furthermore, they promote communication between the residents and thus strengthen the sense of community.

Mit dem 200 Kilometer östlich von Peking gelegenen Projekt transformiert Moshe Safdie seine Entwurfsidee von Habitat 67 in Montreal nun in einen ungleich größeren Maßstab. Die ersten beiden von vier geplanten, stark verdichteten Blöcken reihen sich in einem eigens angelegten Park jeweils im 90-Grad-Winkel aneinander. Zwischen den zueinander versetzt gestapelten Bau-körpern befinden sich große, mit Geschäften gesäumte Öffnungen. Sie schaffen neben umfangreichen Einkaufs-möglichkeiten eine Verbindung zur angrenzenden Strandpromenade. Die Gemeinschaftsterrassen, die die Bauteile verbinden, bieten ebenso wie die abge-treppten privaten Balkone einen direkten Ausblick aufs Meer. Darüber hinaus fördern sie die Kommunikation zwischen den Bewohnern und stärken somit das Gemeinschaftsgefühl.

Nominated Project 2020
Nominiertes Projekt 2020

Skidmore, Owings & Merrill LLP
TIANJIN CTF FINANCE CENTER
Tianjin, China

Architects Architekten **Skidmore, Owings & Merrill LLP, Chicago, IL, USA**
Project architect Projektarchitekt **Brian Lee**
Architects of record Lokale Architekten **Ronald Lu and Partners; East China Architectural Design & Research Institute**
Client Bauherr **New World China Land Limited**
Structural engineers Tragwerksplanung **Skidmore, Owings & Merrill LLP**
MEP Haustechnik **WSP Group Asia**

Height Höhe **530 m**
Stories Geschosse **96**
Site area Grundstücksfläche **27 772 m²**
Building footprint Bebaute Fläche **3718 m²**
Gross floor area Bruttogeschossfläche **389 000 m²**
Structure Konstruktion **Concrete and steel** Beton und Stahl
Completion Fertigstellung **August 2019**
Main use Hauptnutzung **Mixed use comprising office, hotel and apartments** Mischnutzung aus Büros, Hotel und Wohnen

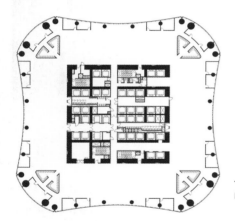

Typical floor plan office
Regelgrundriss Büro

Sustainability:
LEED Gold certification; excellent transport connections; the building shape was optimized by wind tunnel studies, resulting in wind accelerations about half of those of comparable buildings; efficient use of materials and innovative structural system eliminated the need for outriggers and dampers, reducing steel and concrete quantities by 30 respectively 17 percent; optimal building design, a system of inclined columns and simplified connection details resulted in reduced material use with lower production and assembly costs and a shorter construction time; cooling towers are located at the rooftop level at 485 meters above ground, so that the operating efficiency of the system will be at least 15 percent higher than for buildings with standard height and cooling towers at podium level

Nachhaltigkeit:
LEED-Zertifizierung in Gold; hervorragende Verkehrs-anbindung; die Gebäudeform wurde durch Windkanalstudien optimiert, mit dem Ergebnis, dass Windbeschleunigungen nur etwa halb so hoch sind wie bei vergleichbaren Gebäuden; durch effizienten Materialeinsatz und ein innovatives Struktursystem wurden Abstützungen und Dämpfer überflüssig, was eine Reduzierung der Stahl- und Betonmengen um 30 bzw. 17 Prozent zur Folge hatte; optimale Gebäude-konstruktion, ein System geneigter Säulen und vereinfachte Verbindungsdetails führten zu einem reduzierten Materialeinsatz mit geringeren Herstellungs- und Montagekosten und einer verkürzten Bauzeit; Kühltürme befinden sich auf der Dachebene in 485 Metern Höhe über dem Boden, sodass die Betriebs-effizienz des Systems mindestens 15 Prozent höher sein wird als bei Gebäuden mit normaler Höhe und Kühl-türmen auf Sockelhöhe

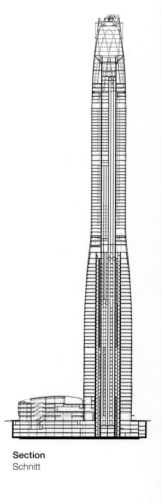

Section
Schnitt

The City of Tianjin connects the capital city of Beijing with the sea and is one of China's commercial centers. Its steadily growing need for space requires the continuous development of formerly peripheral areas. The Tianjin CTF Finance Center not far from the port is the anchor project within the master plan developed by SOM for the Binhai New Area in the east of the city.
Behind a continuous façade, the building brings together various uses, the zoning of which is still visible thanks to technical floors that are permeable to wind. The flowing shape of the tower, which tapers towards the top and rises high above its surroundings, is largely based on factors such as wind loads and earthquake resistance. The enormous experience of the architectural office in this sector together with extensive tests in the wind tunnel ultimately led to an innovative and resource-saving supporting structure consisting of a core within the core and eight inclined main columns.

Die Stadt Tianjin verbindet die Hauptstadt Peking mit dem Meer und ist eines der Handelszentren Chinas. Dessen stetig wachsender Flächenbedarf erfordert die kontinuierliche Entwicklung ehemaliger Randgebiete. Das Tianjin CTF Finance Center unweit des Hafens stellt das Ankerprojekt dar im Rahmen des von SOM entwickelten Masterplans für die Binhai New Area im Osten der Stadt.
Unter einer durchgängigen Fassade vereint das Gebäude die verschiedenen Nutzungen, deren Zonierung durch winddurchlässige Technikgeschosse dennoch ablesbar bleibt. Die fließende Form des sich nach oben verjüngenden und seine Umgebung weit überragenden Turms basiert wesentlich auf Faktoren wie Windlasten und Erdbebensicherheit. Die enorme Erfahrung des Büros auf diesem Sektor sowie umfangreiche Tests im Windkanal führten schlussendlich zu einem innovativen und ressourcenschonenden Tragwerk aus einem Kern im Kern sowie acht schräg verlaufenden Hauptstützen.

Hotel
Hotel

Residential
Wohnen

Office
Büro

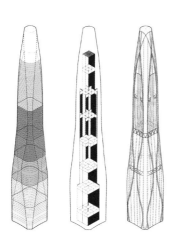

Nominated Project 2020
Nominiertes Projekt 2020

Studio Gang Architects
MIRA
San Francisco, CA, USA

Architects Architekten **Studio Gang Architects,**
Chicago, IL, USA
Project architect Projektarchitekt **Jeanne Gang**
Architects of record Lokale Architekten **Perry**
Architects; Barcelon Jang Architecture
Client Bauherr **Tishman Speyer**
Structural engineers Tragwerksplanung **Magnusson**
Klemencic Associates
MEP Haustechnik **Critchfield Mechanical; Cupertino**
Electrical; Marelich Mechanical; SJ Engineers

Height Höhe **122 m**
Stories Geschosse **39**
Site area Grundstücksfläche **5005 m²**
Building footprint Bebaute Fläche **2731 m²**
Gross floor area Bruttogeschossfläche **41 001 m²**
Structure Konstruktion **Reinforced concrete**
Stahlbeton
Completion Fertigstellung **August 2019**
Main use Hauptnutzung **Residential** Wohnen

Sustainability:
LEED Gold certification (aspired); exceeds California
Title 24 energy standards; increased construction
efficiency, reducing the need for a tower crane on
site and limiting energy consumption and neigh-
borhood impact during construction; infill units are
clad according to the function of interior spaces,
allowing the envelope to achieve more than 50
percent insulating opacity for improved energy
performance; building-wide graywater harvesting
system; VRF cooling system

Nachhaltigkeit:
LEED-Zertifizierung in Gold (angestrebt); übertrifft die
kalifornischen Energiestandards nach Titel 24; erhöhte
Effizienz in der Bauausführung reduziert den Bedarf
an einem Turmdrehkran und verringert den Energieverbrauch und die Auswirkungen auf die Nachbarschaft
während des Baus; Ausfachungen werden entsprechend
der Funktion der Innenräume verkleidet, sodass die
Hülle eine mehr als 50-prozentige isolierende Opazität
zur Verbesserung der Energieeffizienz erreicht; gebäude-
weites Grauwassernutzungssystem; VRF-Kühlsystem

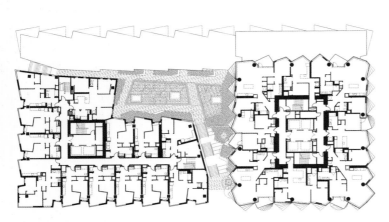

Typical floor plan
Grundriss Regelgeschoss

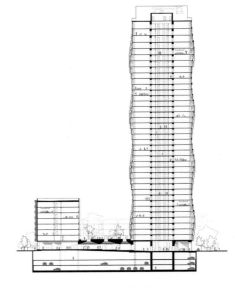

Section
Schnitt

Mira is a residential project in the heart of San
Francisco, just a few blocks away from Bay Bridge
in the Transbay District. 40 percent of the
apartments are available at rents below the local
rent index. The concept responds to the competitive
housing market by offering compact but spacious
apartments. Communal facilities, a central courtyard
and a roof terrace for all residents encourage
encounters. The classic bay window, a familiar motif
in San Francisco, was further developed for the
high-rise building. Turned step by step, the windows
wind their way up around the tower. This makes
each unit a corner apartment with views in different
directions and the best possible lighting and
ventilation. On the ground floor, the bay windows
convey a human scale and serve as sun protection
for the shop windows and lobby.

Mira ist ein Wohnbauprojekt im Herzen San Franciscos,
nur wenige Blocks entfernt von der Bay Bridge im
Transbay District. 40 Prozent der Wohnungen werden
unterhalb des ortsüblichen Mietspiegels angeboten. So
reagiert das Konzept auf den umkämpften Wohnungsmarkt und bietet kompakte, aber trotzdem geräumige
Apartments. Gemeinschaftseinrichtungen, ein zentraler
Hof und eine Dachterrasse für alle Bewohner fördern
Begegnungen. Das klassische Erkerfenster, ein vertrau-
tes Motiv in San Francisco, wurde für das Hochhaus
weiterentwickelt. Schrittweise verdreht winden sich die
Fenster um den Turm in die Höhe. Auf diese Weise wird
jede Wohnung zur Eckwohnung mit Aussicht in verschiedene Richtungen sowie bestmöglicher Belichtung
und Belüftung. Im Erdgeschoss vermitteln die Erker
einen menschlichen Maßstab und dienen als Sonnenschutz für Schaufenster und Lobby.

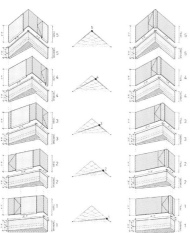

WOHA
SKY GREEN
Taichung, Taiwan

Architects Architekten **WOHA, Singapore** Singapur
Project architects Projektarchitekten **Wong Mun Summ, Richard Hassell, Pearl Chee**
Architects of record Lokale Architekten **Archiman Architects Planners Associates**
Client Bauherr **Golden Jade Construction & Development Corp.**
Structural engineers Tragwerksplanung **DAYAN Engineering Consultant**
MEP Haustechnik **Jin Ding Electrical Machinery Industry Technician's Office**

Height Höhe **104 m**
Stories Geschosse **24**
Site area Grundstücksfläche **4597 m²**
Building footprint Bebaute Fläche **2703 m²**
Gross floor area Bruttogeschossfläche **61 027 m²**
Structure Konstruktion **Reinforced concrete and steel** Stahlbeton und Stahl
Completion Fertigstellung **November 2019**
Main use Hauptnutzung **Residential** Wohnen

Sustainability:
Green-plot ratio of 320 percent; plants include 60 000 trees, shrubs, climbers bringing biodiversity back into the city; automatic irrigation system, rain water harvesting, grey water recycling for plant irrigation to reduce water consumption; greenery acts as an active and living interface between the interior and exterior environment; façade elements passively cool the building; deeply recessed windows additionally facilitate effective shading; natural cross-ventilation

Nachhaltigkeit:
Grünflächenanteil von 320 Prozent; die Bepflanzung umfasst 60 000 Bäume, Sträucher und Kletterpflanzen, die die Artenvielfalt zurück in die Stadt bringen; automatisches Bewässerungssystem, Regenwasser-nutzung, Grauwasserrecycling für die Bewässerung der Pflanzen, zur Reduzierung des Wasserverbrauchs; die Begrünung fungiert als aktive und lebendige Schnittstelle zwischen der internen und externen Umgebung; Fassadenelemente bewirken eine passive Gebäude-kühlung; tief zurückgesetzte Fenster ermöglichen zusätzlich eine effektive Beschattung; natürliche Querlüftung

Typical floor plans with skygardens
Grundriss Regelgeschosse mit Himmelsgärten

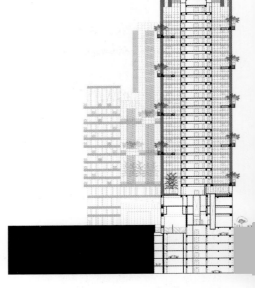

Section
Schnitt

Inspired by the WOHA exhibition *Breathing Architecture* (curated by Deutsches Architekturmuseum, DAM) hosted in Taichung, the client Golden Jade commissioned the office with the first sustainable and green mixed-use project in Taiwan's second largest city.
Sky Green, with its two earthquake-resistant towers, well-ventilated common areas, and botanical diversity, already serves as a reference project for future urban development. A further 27 construction projects are already oriented towards the green typology of this development, which is designed to improve the climate and quality of life in the city. The architects are thus demonstrating that their Singaporean tropical model of the skyscraper can also be transferred to other regions of the world.

Inspiriert durch die in Taichung gastierende WOHA-Ausstellung „Breathing Architecture" (kuratiert vom Deutsches Architekturmuseum), beauftragte der Bauherr Golden Jade das Büro mit dem ersten nachhaltig begrünten Mixed-Use-Projekt in der zweitgrößten Stadt Taiwans.
Sky Green mit seinen beiden erdbebensicheren Türmen, den durchlüfteten Gemeinschaftsflächen und der botanischen Vielfalt dient der Stadtplanung schon jetzt als Referenzprojekt für die zukünftige Stadtentwicklung. Bereits 27 weitere Bauvorhaben orientieren sich an der grünen Typologie des Projekts, die zur Verbesserung des Klimas und der Lebensqualität in der Stadt beitragen soll. Somit belegen die Architekten, dass ihr singapurisch tropisches Modell des Hochhauses auch auf andere Regionen der Welt übertragbar ist.

Zaha Hadid Architects
**MORPHEUS HOTEL & RESORTS
AT CITY OF DREAMS**
Macau, China

Architects Architekten **Zaha Hadid Architects,
London, UK** Großbritannien
Project architects Projektarchitekten **Zaha Hadid,
Patrik Schumacher, Viviana Muscettola, Michele
Pasca di Magliano**
Architects of record Lokale Architekten **Leigh &
Orange, CAA City Planning & Engineering
Consultants**
Client Bauherr **Melco Resorts & Entertainment**
Structural engineers Tragwerksplanung **Buro Happold**
MEP Haustechnik **J. Roger Preston**

Height Höhe **160 m**
Stories Geschosse **42**
Site area Grundstücksfläche **5000 m²**
Building footprint Bebaute Fläche **5000 m²**
Gross floor area Bruttogeschossfläche **147 860 m²**
Structure Konstruktion **Reinforced concrete and steel**
Stahlbeton und Stahl
Completion Fertigstellung **June** Juni **2018**
Main use Hauptnutzung **Hotel**

Sustainability:
Integration of existing abandoned foundations; high-performance glazing to minimize solar gain; exoskeleton provides additional screening from the sun; the atrium's middle areas are not air conditioned, only zones used by guests and staff; exterior panels were produced locally to the highest international standards, reducing unnecessary transportation and making full use of local expertise and equipment; air-handling units with high-efficiency, variable-speed, water-cooled chillers, and thermal wheel heat exchangers to recover energy from exhaust air; a water-to-water heat pump pre-heats domestic water, while the hotel's smart building management system responds in real time to usage and environmental conditions to minimize energy consumption

Nachhaltigkeit:
Einbeziehung vorhandener ungenutzter Fundamente; Hochleistungsverglasung zur Minimierung der Sonneneinstrahlung; Exoskelett bietet zusätzlichen Sonnenschutz; die Mittelzonen des Atriums sind nicht klimatisiert, sondern nur die von Gästen und Personal genutzten Bereiche; die Außenverkleidung wurde lokal gefertigt und entspricht höchsten internationalen Standards, wodurch unnötige Transporte reduziert und lokales Fachwissen und Ausrüstung in vollem Umfang genutzt wurden; Lüftungsgeräte mit hocheffizienten, wassergekühlten Kühlaggregaten mit variabler Drehzahl und Rotationswärmetauschern zur Energierückgewinnung aus der Abluft; eine Wasser/Wasser-Wärmepumpe wärmt Brauchwasser vor, während das intelligente Building-Management-System des Hotels in Echtzeit auf Nutzungs- und Umweltbedingungen reagiert, um den Energieverbrauch zu minimieren

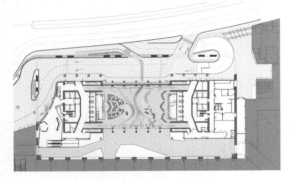

Site plan
Lageplan

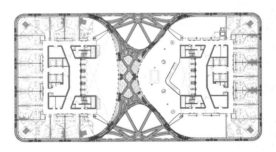

Floor plan level 25
Grundriss 25. Obergeschoss

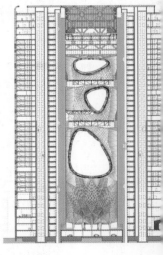

Section
Schnitt

As part of a large amusement resort with casino and shopping center, the twin towers of the Morpheus Hotel rise above the rectangular foundation originally built for another high-rise project. They are connected via the roof terrace, two bridges, and a shared multi-story entrance hall. The individual building units are enclosed by a façade consisting of an exoskeleton and blue mirror glass in a way that they seem to merge. Restaurants, bars, and lounges with opulently sculptural interior design are accommodated in flowing, column-free sequences of rooms, connecting the total of 770 hotel rooms and suites along the exterior walls of the building.

Als Teil eines großen Vergnügungsresorts mit Casino und Einkaufszentrum erheben sich die beiden Doppeltürme des Hotels Morpheus über dem ursprünglich für ein anderes Hochhausprojekt gebauten rechteckigen Fundament. Sie sind über die Dachterrasse, zwei Brücken sowie eine gemeinsame, mehrgeschossige Eingangshalle miteinander verbunden. Dabei werden die einzelnen Bauteile von einer Fassade, bestehend aus einem Exoskelett und blauem Spiegelglas, so umschlossen, dass sie scheinbar verschmelzen. In fließenden, stützenfreien Raumfolgen befinden sich hier Restaurants, Bars und Lounges mit opulent skulpturaler Innenarchitektur, die die insgesamt 770 Zimmer und Suiten entlang der Außenwände des Gebäudes miteinander verbinden.

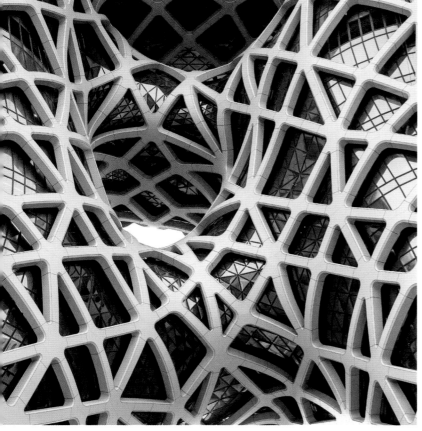

Winners of the International Highrise Award
Preisträger Internationaler Hochhaus Preis
2004–2018

Award Winner Preisträger **2018**
TORRE REFORMA Mexico City Mexiko-Stadt,
Mexico Mexiko
Architects Architekten **L. Benjamín Romano (LBR&A),
Mexico City** Mexiko-Stadt, **Mexico** Mexiko
Client Bauherr **Fondo Hexa, S.A. de C.V.**

Award Winner Preisträger **2016**
VIA 57 WEST New York, NY, USA
Architects Architekten **BIG – Bjarke Ingels Group,
Copenhagen** Kopenhagen, **Denmark** Dänemark/**New
York, NY, USA**
Local architects Lokale Architekten **SLCE Architects,
New York**
Client Bauherr **The Durst Organization, New York**

Award Winner Preisträger **2014**
BOSCO VERTICALE Milan Mailand, **Italy** Italien
Architects Architekten **Boeri Studio, Milan** Mailand,
Italy Italien
Client Bauherr **Hines Italia SGR S.p.A., Milan** Mailand

Award Winner Preisträger **2012**
1 BLIGH STREET Sydney, Australia Australien
Architects Architekten **ingenhoven architects,
Dusseldorf** Düsseldorf, **Germany** Deutschland;
Architectus, Sydney, Australia Australien
Client Bauherr **DEXUS Property Group; DEXUS
Wholesale Property Fund; Cbus Property, Sydney
(all** alle)

Award Winner Preisträger **2010**
THE MET Bangkok, Thailand
Architects Architekten **WOHA, Singapore** Singapur
Associated architects Assoziierte Architekten **Tandem
Architects (2001) Co. Ltd., Bangkok**
Client Bauherr **Pebble Bay Thailand Co. Ltd., Bangkok**

Award Winner Preisträger **2008**
HEARST HEADQUARTERS New York, NY, USA
Architects Architekten **Foster + Partners, London, UK**
Großbritannien
Architects of record/shell and core Lokale
Architekten/Rohbau **Adamson Associates, Toronto**
Client Bauherr **Hearst Corporation, New York**

Award Winner Preisträger **2006**
TORRE AGBAR Barcelona, Spain Spanien
Architects Architekten **Ateliers Jean Nouvel, Paris,
France** Frankreich
Client Bauherr **Layetana Developments, Barcelona**

Award Winner Preisträger **2004**
DE HOFTOREN The Hague Den Haag, **Netherlands**
Niederlande
Architects Architekten **Kohn Pedersen Fox
Associates, London, UK** Großbritannien
Client Bauherr **ING Vastgoed, The Hague** Den Haag

TORRE REFORMA
2018 Mexico City Mexiko-Stadt,
Mexico Mexiko

THE MET
2010 Bangkok, Thailand

VIA 57 WEST
2016 New York, NY, USA

BOSCO VERTICALE
2014 **Milan** Mailand, **Italy** Italien

1 BLIGH STREET
2012 Sydney, **Australia** Australien

HEARST HEADQUARTERS
2008 New York, NY, USA

TORRE AGBAR
2006 **Barcelona, Spain** Spanien

DE HOFTOREN
2004 **The Hague** Den Haag,
Netherlands Niederlande

List of Projects Projektliste
The International Highrise Award Internationaler Hochhaus Preis
2004–2020

3D/International, Houston, TX, USA
Carl B. Stokes Federal Courthouse, Cleveland, OH, USA
Submission Einreichung **2004**

ABB Architekten, Frankfurt am Main, Germany
Bocom Financial Towers, Shanghai, China
Submission Einreichung **2004**

Aedas, London, UK
Al Bahr Towers, Abu Dhabi, UAE
Nomination Nominierung **2014**

Aflalo & Gasperini Arquitectos, São Paulo, Brazil
Ventura Corporate Tower, Rio de Janeiro, Brazil
Nomination Nominierung **2012**

AL_A, London, UK
Central Embassy, Bangkok, Thailand
Nomination Nominierung **2018**

Amateur Architecture Studio, Hangzhou, China
Vertical Courtyard, Hangzhou, China
Nomination Nominierung **2008**

Andrea Maffei Architects, Milan, Italy
Allianz Tower, Milan, Italy
Nomination Nominierung **2016**

Arata Isozaki & Associates, Tokyo, Japan
Allianz Tower, Milan, Italy
Nomination Nominierung **2016**

Arc Studio Architecture + Urbanism, Singapore
Pinnacle@Duxton, Singapore
Finalist 2012

Architectus, Sydney, Australia
1 Bligh Street, Sydney, Australia
Prize Winner Preisträger **2012**

Arquitectonica International Corporation, Miami, FL, USA
Landmark East, Hong Kong
Nomination Nominierung **2010**
Torun Tower, Istanbul, Turkey
Nomination Nominierung **2016**

Atelier Christian Portzamparc, Paris, France
One57, New York, NY, USA
Nomination Nominierung **2014**

Ateliers Jean Nouvel, Paris, France
Torre Agbar, Barcelona, Spain
Prize Winner Preisträger **2006**
Doha Tower, Doha, Qatar
Nomination Nominierung **2014**
One Central Park, Sydney, Australia
Finalist 2014
Renaissance Barcelona Fira Hotel, Barcelona, Spain
Finalist 2014
Le Nouvel Ardmore, Singapore
Nomination Nominierung **2016**

Le Nouvel KLCC, Kuala Lumpur, Malaysia
Nomination Nominierung **2018**
La Marseillaise, Marseille, France
Nomination Nominierung **2020**

Atkins, London, UK
Bahrain World Trade Center, Manama, Bahrain
Nomination Nominierung **2008**
Landmark 81, Ho Chi Minh City, Vietnam
Nomination Nominierung **2020**

Audrius Ambrasas Architects, Vilnius, Lithuania
Europa Tower, Vilnius, Lithuania
Submission Einreichung **2004**

Baumschlager Eberle, Lustenau, Austria
PopMoma, Beijing, China
Nomination Nominierung **2008**

BIG – Bjarke Ingels Group, Copenhagen/New York, NY, Denmark, USA
VIA 57 West, New York, NY, USA
Prize Winner Preisträger **2016**
Omniturm, Frankfurt am Main, Germany
Finalist 2020
Shenzhen Energy Headquarters, Shenzhen, China
Nomination Nominierung **2020**

Boeri Studio, Milan, Italy
Bosco Verticale, Milan, Italy
Prize Winner Preisträger **2014**

Building Design (Pvt) Ltd., Colombo, Sri Lanka
HNB Towers, Colombo, Sri Lanka
Submission Einreichung **2004**

Buro Ole Scheeren, Beijing, China
CCTV Headquarters, Beijing, China
Nomination Nominierung **2014**
DUO, Singapore
Nomination Nominierung **2018**
MahaNakhon, Bangkok, Thailand
Finalist 2018

C. Y. Lee & Partners, Taipei, Taiwan
Taipei 101, Taipei, Taiwan
Nomination Nominierung **2006**

Carlos Zapata Studio, New York, NY, USA
Bitexco Financial Tower, Ho Chi Minh City, Vietnam
Nomination Nominierung **2012**

CCDI Group, Shenzhen, China
Shenzhen Baidu Headquarters, Shenzhen, China
Nomination Nominierung **2020**

CetraRuddy Architecture, New York, NY, USA
One Madison Park, New York, NY, USA
Nomination Nominierung **2012**
ARO, New York, NY, USA
Nomination Nominierung **2020**

Cook + Fox Architects LLP, New York, NY, USA
The Bank of America Tower, New York, NY, USA
Nomination Nominierung **2010**

Coop Himmelb(l)au, Vienna, Austria
ECB – European Central Bank, Frankfurt am Main, Germany
Nomination Nominierung **2016**

Cox Architecture, Sydney, Australia
Metro Residences Chatswood, Sydney, Australia
Nomination Nominierung **2016**

(designed by) Erick van Egeraat, Rotterdam, Netherlands
Mercury City Tower, Moscow, Russia
Nomination Nominierung **2012**

Dam & Partners Architecten, Amsterdam, Netherlands
Maastoren, Rotterdam, Netherlands
Nomination Nominierung **2010**

David Chipperfield Architects, Berlin, Germany
Amorepacific Headquarters, Seoul, South Korea
Nomination Nominierung **2018**

Delugan Meissl Associated Architects, Vienna, Austria
Delugan Meissl Tower, Vienna, Austria
Finalist 2006

Diller Scofidio + Renfro, New York, NY, USA
15 Hudson Yards, New York, NY, USA
Nomination Nominierung **2020**

Dina Ammar – Avraham Curiel Architects, Haifa, Israel
The Sail Tower, Haifa, Israel
Submission Einreichung **2004**

Dominique Perrault Architecture, Paris, France
ME Barcelona Hotel, Barcelona, Spain
Nomination Nominierung **2010**
Fukoku Tower, Osaka, Japan
Nomination Nominierung **2012**
DC Tower I, Vienna, Austria
Nomination Nominierung **2014**
5th Extension of the European Court of Justice, Luxembourg
Nomination Nominierung **2020**

Donovan Hill, Brisbane, Australia
Santos Place, Brisbane, Australia
Nomination Nominierung **2010**

Ellerbe Becket, Minneapolis, MN, USA
Kingdom Centre, Riyadh, Saudi Arabia
Submission Einreichung **2004**

EMBA_Estudi Massip-Bosch Arquitectes, Barcelona, Spain
Torre Telefónica Diagonal ZeroZero, Barcelona, Spain
Nomination Nominierung **2012**

Estudio de Arquitectura Alonso Balaguer SLP, Barcelona, Spain
Bacatá Tower, Bogotá, Colombia
Nomination Nominierung **2020**

Fender Katsalidis Architects, Melbourne, Australia
Eureka Tower, Melbourne, Australia
Nomination Nominierung **2008**

Foster + Partners, London, UK
30 St Mary Axe, London, UK
Finalist 2004
Deutsche Bank Place, Sydney, Australia
Nomination Nominierung **2006**
Hearst Headquarters, New York, NY, USA
Prize Winner Preisträger **2008**
Regent Place, Sydney, Australia
Nomination Nominierung **2008**
The Willis Building, London, UK
Nomination Nominierung **2008**

Jameson House, Vancouver, Canada
Nomination Nominierung **2012**
The Index, Dubai, UAE
Nomination Nominierung **2012**
The Troika, Kuala Lumpur, Malaysia
Finalist 2012
The Bow, Calgary, Canada
Nomination Nominierung **2014**
Burj Mohammed Bin Rashid + World Trade Center,
Abu Dhabi, UAE
Nomination Nominierung **2016**
South Beach, Singapore
Nomination Nominierung **2016**
UN Plaza, New York, NY, USA
Nomination Nominierung **2016**
The Bund Finance Center, Shanghai, China
Nomination Nominierung **2018**
Comcast Technology Center, Philadelphia, PA, USA
Nomination Nominierung **2020**
National Bank of Kuwait (NBK Tower), Kuwait City, Kuwait
Nomination Nominierung **2020**

Francis-Jones Morehen Thorp, Sydney, Australia
EY Centre, Sydney, Australia
Nomination Nominierung **2018**

Frank Williams & Associates, New York, NY, USA
Mercury City Tower, Moscow, Russia
Nomination Nominierung **2014**

Gatermann + Schossig, Cologne, Germany
KölnTriangle, Cologne, Germany
Nomination Nominierung **2006**

Gehry Partners LLP, Los Angeles, CA, USA
Eight Spruce Street, New York, NY, USA
Finalist 2012

Gensler, San Francisco, CA, USA
Shanghai Tower, Shanghai, China
Nomination Nominierung **2016**

Gerber Architekten, Dortmund, Germany
RWE Tower, Dortmund, Germany
Nomination Nominierung **2006**

Gigon/Guyer Architekten, Zurich, Switzerland
Prime Tower, Zurich, Switzerland
Nomination Nominierung **2012**

GKK+Architekten, Berlin, Germany
Hauptverwaltung Süddeutscher Verlag, Munich, Germany
Nomination Nominierung **2010**

gmp Architekten von Gerkan, Marg und Partner, Hamburg, Germany
Guangzhou Development Central Building, Guangzhou, China
Nomination Nominierung **2006**
Wanda Plaza, Beijing, China
Nomination Nominierung **2008**
Neue Deutsche Bank Towers (revitalization), Frankfurt, Germany
Sp. Mention Bes. Anerkennung **2012**
Bund SOHO, Shanghai, China
Nomination Nominierung **2016**
Greenland Central Plaza, Zhengzhou, China
Nomination Nominierung **2018**
Nanjing Financial City, Nanjing, China
Nomination Nominierung **2018**
Poly Greenland Plaza, Shanghai, China
Nomination Nominierung **2020**

Goettsch Partners, Chicago, IL, USA
150 North Riverside, Chicago, IL, USA
Nomination Nominierung **2018**

GRAFT, Berlin, Germany
Luxe Lake Towers, Chengdu, China
Nomination Nominierung **2020**

Gruber + Kleine-Kraneburg Architekten, Frankfurt, Germany
TaunusTurm, Frankfurt, Germany
Nomination Nominierung **2014**

Harry Gugger Studio, Basel, Switzerland
The Exchange, Vancouver, Canada
Nomination Nominierung **2018**

Harry Seidler and Associates, Sydney, Australia
The Cove, Sydney, Australia
Finalist 2004
Riparian Plaza, Brisbane, Australia
Nomination Nominierung **2006**
Meriton Tower, Sydney, Australia
Nomination Nominierung **2008**

Heatherwick Studio, London, UK
The Bund Finance Center, Shanghai, China
Nomination Nominierung **2018**
EDEN, Singapore
Finalist 2020

Heller Manus Architects, San Francisco, CA, USA
181 Fremont, San Francisco, CA, USA
Nomination Nominierung **2018**

Herzog & de Meuron, Basel, Switzerland
56 Leonard Street, New York, NY, USA
Nomination Nominierung **2018**
Beirut Terraces, Beirut, Lebanon
Finalist 2018

Ian Moore Architects, Manchester, UK
Air Apartments, Broadbeach/QLD, Australia
Nomination Nominierung **2008**

Ian Simpson Architects, Manchester, UK
Beetham Hilton Tower, Manchester, UK
Nomination Nominierung **2008**
Holloway Circus, Birmingham, UK
Nomination Nominierung **2008**

ingenhoven architects, Dusseldorf, Germany
Uptown München, Munich, Germany
Nomination Nominierung **2006**
Breezé Tower, Osaka, Japan
Nomination Nominierung **2010**
1 Bligh Street, Sydney, Australia
Prize Winner Preisträger **2012**
Marina One, Singapore
Nomination Nominierung **2018**

JAHN, Chicago, IL, USA
Cosmopolitan Twarda 2/4, Warsaw, Poland
Nomination Nominierung **2016**
50 West, New York, NY, USA
Nomination Nominierung **2018**

John Lee/Michael Timchula Architects, New York, NY, USA
Shenzhen World Trade Center, Shenzhen, China
Submission Einreichung **2004**

Johnson Fain, Los Angeles, CA, USA
Constellation Palace, Los Angeles, CA, USA
Submission Einreichung **2004**

J.S.K. International Architekten und Ingenieure, Frankfurt, Germany
Tornado Tower, Doha, Qatar
Nomination Nominierung **2010**

Kallmann Mckinnell & Wood Architects, Boston, MA, USA
Carl B. Stokes Federal Courthouse, Cleveland, OH, USA
Submission Einreichung **2004**

KCAP Architects & Planners, Rotterdam, Netherlands
The Red Apple, Rotterdam, Netherlands
Nomination Nominierung **2010**

Kohn Pedersen Fox Associates PC, New York, NY, USA
De Hoftoren, The Hague, Netherlands
Prize Winner Preisträger **2004**
Roppongi Hills Mori Tower, Tokyo, Japan
Submission Einreichung **2004**
Adia Headquarters, Abu Dhabi, UAE
Nomination Nominierung **2008**
International Commerce Center, Hong Kong
Nomination Nominierung **2010**
Shanghai World Financial Center, Shanghai, China
Finalist 2010
Ventura Corporate Tower, Rio de Janeiro, Brazil
Nomination Nominierung **2012**
Lotte World Tower, Seoul, South Korea
Nomination Nominierung **2018**
Ping An Finance Centre, Shenzhen, China
Nomination Nominierung **2018**
China Resources Tower, Shenzhen, China
Nomination Nominierung **2020**
MGM Cotai, Macau, China
Nomination Nominierung **2020**
Robinson Tower, Singapore
Nomination Nominierung **2020**

KSP Jürgen Engel Architekten, Frankfurt, Germany
WestendDuo, Frankfurt, Germany
Sp. Mention Bes. Anerkennung **2008**
Palais Quartier Office Tower, Frankfurt, Germany
Nomination Nominierung **2010**

Kuwabara Payne McKenna Blumberg Architects, Toronto, Canada
Manitoba Hydro Place, Winnipeg, Canada
Nomination Nominierung **2010**

L. Benjamín Romano (LBR&A), Mexico City, Mexico
Torre Reforma, Mexico City, Mexico
Prize Winner Preisträger **2018**

Legorreta, Mexico City, Mexico
Torre BBVA Bancomer, Mexico City, Mexico
Nomination Nominierung **2016**
Miyana, Torre Chapulín, Mexico City, Mexico
Nomination Nominierung **2020**

Louis Karlsberger & Associates, Columbus, OH, USA
Carl B. Stokes Federal Courthouse, Cleveland, OH, USA
Submission Einreichung **2004**

M. M. Posokhin, Moscow, Russia
Mercury City Tower, Moscow, Russia
Nomination Nominierung **2012**

MAD Architects, Beijing, China
Absolute World Towers, Mississauga, Canada
Finalist 2012
Sheraton Huzhou Hot Spring Resort, Huzhou, China
Nomination Nominierung 2014
Fake Hills (Part 1), Beihai, China
Nomination Nominierung 2016
Chaoyang Park Plaza, Beijing, China
Finalist 2018

Magnus Kaminiarz & Cie. Architektur, Frankfurt am Main, Germany
Grand Tower, Frankfurt am Main, Germany
Nomination Nominierung 2020

Maki & Associates, Tokyo, Japan
4 World Trade Center, New York, NY, USA
Finalist 2016

Mario Bellini Architects, Milan, Italy
Neue Deutsche Bank Towers, Frankfurt, Germany
Sp. Mention Bes. Anerkennung 2012

Mario Botta Architetto, Mendrisio, Switzerland
Kyobo Gangnam Tower, Seoul, South Korea
Finalist 2004

Mass Studies, Seoul, South Korea
Missing Matrix Building, Seoul, South Korea
Finalist 2008
S-trenue: Bundle Matrix, Seoul, South Korea
Nomination Nominierung 2010

Mecanoo Architecten, Rotterdam, Netherlands
Montevideo, Rotterdam, Netherlands
Finalist 2006

Meixner Schlüter Wendt, Frankfurt am Main, Germany
Neuer Henninger Turm, Frankfurt, Germany
Nomination Nominierung 2018

Mitsubishi Jisho Sekkei Inc., Tokyo, Japan
Breezé Tower, Osaka, Japan
Nomination Nominierung 2010

Morger & Degelo, Marques, Basel, Switzerland
Basler Messeturm, Basel, Switzerland
Submission Einreichung 2004

Morphosis, Culver City, CA, USA
Casablanca Finance City Tower, Casablanca, Morocco
Nomination Nominierung 2020

Murphy/Jahn Architects, Chicago, IL, USA
Post Tower, Bonn, Germany
Submission Einreichung 2004
Highlight Towers, Munich, Germany
Nomination Nominierung 2006
Veer Towers, Las Vegas, NV, USA
Nomination Nominierung 2012

MVSA – Meyer en Van Schooten Architecten, Amsterdam, Netherlands
New Babylon, The Hague, Netherlands
Nomination Nominierung 2012

NBBJ, Seattle, WA, USA
Tencent Seafront Headquarters, Shenzhen, China
Nomination Nominierung 2018

Novotny Mähner Assoziierte, Offenbach, Germany
Gallileo, Frankfurt, Germany
Submission Einreichung 2004

nps tchoban voss, Hamburg, Germany
Federation Towers, Moscow, Russia
Nomination Nominierung 2016

OMA Office for Metropolitan Architecture, Rotterdam / Beijing, Netherlands/China
TVCC – Television Cultural Center, Beijing, China
Finalist 2008
Shenzhen Stock Exchange, Shenzhen, China
Nomination Nominierung 2010
CCTV Headquarters, Beijing, China
Nomination Nominierung 2014
De Rotterdam, Rotterdam, Netherlands
Finalist 2014
MahaNakhon, Bangkok, Thailand
Finalist 2018
Norra Tornen – Innovationen, Stockholm, Sweden
Prize Winner Preisträger 2018

Paul Davis & Partners, London, UK
Grosvenor Place, Hong Kong
Submission Einreichung 2004

Pei Cobb Freed & Partners Architects LLP, New York, NY, USA
Torre Espacio, Madrid, Spain
Nomination Nominierung 2008

Pelli Clarke Pelli Architects, New Haven, CT, USA
Two International Finance Center, Hong Kong
Nomination Nominierung 2006
Torre Costanera, Santiago, Chile
Nomination Nominierung 2014
Salesforce Tower, San Francisco, CA, USA
Nomination Nominierung 2018

Perkins + Will, Chicago, IL, USA
235 West Van Buren, Chicago, IL, USA
Nomination Nominierung 2010

Prof. Christoph Mäckler Architekten, Frankfurt, Germany
OpernTurm, Frankfurt, Germany
Nomination Nominierung 2010
Zoofenster – Waldorf Astoria Berlin, Berlin, Germany
Nomination Nominierung 2014

querkraft architekten, Vienna, Austria
Citygate Tower & Leopold Tower, Vienna, Austria
Nomination Nominierung 2016

R&AS Rubio & Álvarez-Sala, Madrid, Spain
Torre SyV, Madrid, Spain
Nomination Nominierung 2008

Rafael de La-Hoz Arquitectos, Madrid, Spain
Las Torres de Hércules, Los Barrios, Spain
Nomination Nominierung 2010

Rafael Viñoly Architects, New York, NY, USA
432 Park Avenue, New York, NY, USA
Finalist 2016

NEMA Chicago, Chicago, IL, USA
Nomination Nominierung 2020

Rapp & Rapp, Amsterdam, Netherlands
De Kroon, The Hague, Netherlands
Nomination Nominierung **2014**

Reiser + Umemoto, RUR Architecture PC, New York, NY, USA
O-14, Dubai, UAE
Nomination Nominierung **2010**

Renzo Piano Building Workshop, Genoa, Italy
New York Times Building, New York, NY, USA
Finalist 2008
The Shard London Bridge Tower, London, UK
Nomination Nominierung **2014**
Grattacielo Intesa Sanpaolo, Turin, Italy
Nomination Nominierung **2016**
Tribunal de Paris, Paris, France
Nomination Nominierung **2018**

Research Architecture Design Ltd., Hong Kong
SK Telecom Headquarters, Seoul, South Korea
Nomination Nominierung **2006**

Richard Meier & Partners Architects, New York, NY, USA
Rothschild Tower, Tel Aviv, Israel
Nomination Nominierung **2016**
Torres Cuarzo, Mexico City, Mexico
Nomination Nominierung **2020**

Richard Rogers Partnership, London, UK
Hesperia Hotel and Conference Center, L'Hospitalet/Barcelona, Spain
Nomination Nominierung **2008**

Riken Yamamoto & Field Shop, Yokohama, Japan
Jian Wai Soho, Beijing, China
Finalist 2006

Robert A. M. Stern Architects LLP, New York, NY, USA
Comcast Center, Philadelphia, PA, USA
Nomination Nominierung **2010**

Roberto Perez-Guerras Architects, Madrid, Spain
Neguri Gane, Benidorm, Spain
Submission Einreichung **2004**

Rocco Design Architects Ltd., Hong Kong
One Beijing Road, Hong Kong
Submission Einreichung **2004**

Rogers Stirk Harbour & Partners, London, UK
8 Chifley Square, Sydney, Australia
Nomination Nominierung **2014**
The Leadenhall, London, UK
Nomination Nominierung **2014**
Torre BBVA Bancomer, Mexico City, Mexico
Nomination Nominierung **2016**
3 World Trade Center, New York, NY, USA
Nomination Nominierung **2020**

SAA Schweger Associated Architects, Hamburg, Germany
Federation Towers, Moscow, Russia
Nomination Nominierung **2016**

Safdie Architects, Somerville, MA, USA
SkyHabitat, Singapore
Finalist 2016
Golden Dream Bay, Qinhuangdao, China
Nomination Nominierung **2020**

Santiago Calatrava LLC, Zurich, Switzerland
HSB Turning Torso, Malmö, Sweden
Finalist 2006

SCDA Architects, Singapore
SkyTerrace @ Dawson, Singapore
Nomination Nominierung **2016**
Echelon, Singapore
Nomination Nominierung **2018**

schneider + schumacher, Frankfurt, Germany
Westhafen Tower, Frankfurt, Germany
Submission Einreichung **2004**
Silver Tower (revitalization), Frankfurt, Germany
Nomination Nominierung **2010**

SHoP Architects, New York, NY, USA
461 Dean Street, New York, NY, USA
Nomination Nominierung **2018**
American Copper Buildings, New York, NY, USA
Nomination Nominierung **2018**

SimpsonHaugh, London, UK
Dollar Bay, London, UK
Nomination Nominierung **2018**

Skidmore, Owings & Merrill LLP, Chicago, IL, USA
Tower Palace III, Seoul, South Korea
Nomination Nominierung **2006**
7 World Trade Center, New York, NY, USA
Nomination Nominierung **2008**
Burj Khalifa, Dubai, UAE
Sp. Mention Bes. Anerkennung **2010**
The Broadgate Tower, London, UK
Nomination Nominierung **2010**
Trump International Hotel & Tower, Chicago, IL, USA
Nomination Nominierung **2010**
Tianjin Global Financial Center, Tianjin, China
Nomination Nominierung **2012**
Cayan Tower, Dubai, UAE
Nomination Nominierung **2014**
Pearl River Tower, Guangzhou, China
Nomination Nominierung **2014**
1 World Trade Center, New York, NY, USA
Nomination Nominierung **2016**
Baccarat Hotel & Residences, New York, NY, USA
Nomination Nominierung **2016**
Jiangxi Nanchang Greenland Central Plaza, Nanchang, China
Nomination Nominierung **2016**
Poly International Plaza, Beijing, China
Nomination Nominierung **2018**
The Lexicon, London, UK
Nomination Nominierung **2018**
The Stratford, London, UK
Finalist 2020
Tianjin CTF Finance Centre, Tianjin, China
Nomination Nominierung **2020**

Somdoon Architects, Bangkok, Thailand
Ideo Morph 38, Bangkok, Thailand
Nomination Nominierung **2014**

Steidle + Partner, Munich, Germany
Chaowei Men, Beijing, China
Nomination Nominierung **2008**

Steven Holl Architects, New York, NY, USA
Sliced Porosity Block – Raffles City Chengdu, Chengdu, China
Finalist 2014

Studio Daniel Libeskind, New York, NY, USA
Reflections at Keppel Bay, Singapore
Nomination Nominierung **2012**

Studio Gang Architects Ltd., Chicago, IL, USA
Aqua Tower, Chicago, IL, USA
Finalist 2010
MIRA, San Francisco, CA, USA
Nomination Nominierung **2020**

T. R. Hamzah & Yeang Sdn. Bhd., Ampang Selanger, Malaysia
Singapore National Library, Singapore
Nomination Nominierung **2006**

Tabanlioglu Architects, Istanbul, Turkey
Sapphire, Istanbul, Turkey
Nomination Nominierung **2012**

Tago Architects, Istanbul, Turkey
Dumankaya Ikon, Istanbul, Turkey
Nomination Nominierung **2014**

Takenaka Corporation, Osaka, Japan
Abeno Harukas, Osaka, Japan
Nomination Nominierung **2016**

Tange Associates, Tokyo, Japan
Mode Gakuen Cocoon Tower, Tokyo, Japan
Finalist 2010
One Raffles Place Tower 2, Singapore
Nomination Nominierung **2012**

Tectum Architects, Riga, Latvia
Hansabanka Central Office, Riga, Latvia
Nomination Nominierung **2006**

TEN Arquitectos, New York, NY, USA
Mercedes House, New York, NY, USA
Nomination Nominierung **2014**

TFP Farrells, London, UK
KK 100, Shenzhen, China
Nomination Nominierung **2012**

Toyo Ito & Associates, Tokyo, Japan
CapitaGreen, Singapore
Nomination Nominierung **2016**

UN Studio, Amsterdam, Netherlands
Ardmore Residence, Singapore
Nomination Nominierung **2014**
Raffles City, Hangzhou, China
Nomination Nominierung **2018**
The Scotts Tower, Singapore
Nomination Nominierung **2018**

Valode & Pistre Architects, Paris, France
T1 Tower, Paris, France
Nomination Nominierung **2010**

Wilkinson Eyre Architects, London, UK
Guangzhou International Finance Center, Guangzhou, China
Nomination Nominierung **2012**

Wingårdh Arkitektenkontor AB, Gothenburg, Sweden
Victoria Tower, Stockholm, Sweden
Nomination Nominierung **2012**

WOHA, Singapore
Newton Suites, Singapore
Finalist 2008
The Met, Bangkok, Thailand
Prize Winner Preisträger **2010**
SkyVille @ Dawson, Singapore
Finalist 2016
Huaku Sky Garden, Taipei, Taiwan
Nomination Nominierung **2018**
Oasia Hotel Downtown, Singapore
Finalist 2018
Sky Green, Taichung, Taiwan
Nomination Nominierung **2020**

Zaha Hadid Architects, London, UK
CMA CGM Head Office Tower, Marseille, France
Nomination Nominierung **2012**
D'Leedon, Singapore
Nomination Nominierung **2016**
Wangjing SOHO, Beijing, China
Nomination Nominierung **2016**
Generali Tower, Milan, Italy
Nomination Nominierung **2018**
Nanjing International Cultural Centre, Nanjing, China
Nomination Nominierung **2018**
Leeza SOHO, Beijing, China
Finalist 2020
Morpheus Hotel & Resorts at City of Dreams, Macau, China
Nomination Nominierung **2020**

Imprint Project Coordination
Impressum Projektkoordination

Stadt Frankfurt am Main

DAM Deutsches Architekturmuseum
Peter Cachola Schmal, Director Direktor
Peter Körner, Coordination Koordination
Stefanie Lampe, Coordination Koordination
Jonas Malzahn, Coordination Koordination
Brita Köhler, Anna Wegmann, Public Relations
Öffentlichkeitsarbeit
Inka Plechaty, Jacqueline Brauer, Administration
Verwaltung

Department for Culture and Science
Dezernat Kultur und Wissenschaft
Jana Kremin, Press Officer and Head of Public
Relations Pressesprecherin und Leiterin der
Öffentlichkeitsarbeit

DekaBank
Silke Schuster-Müller, Head of Corporate Social
Responsibility Leiterin Gesellschaftliches Engagement
Valery Trosdorf, Corporate Social Responsibility
Gesellschaftliches Engagement
Björn Korschinowski, Head of Corporate
Communications Leiter Unternehmenskommunikation
Dr. Daniela Gniss, Press Officer Referentin
Unternehmenskommunikation
Theresa Sattler, Project Manager Events & Fairs
Projektleiterin Veranstaltungen & Messen

Event organization Veranstaltungsorganisation
Jazzunique GmbH, Frankfurt am Main
Jesper Götsch, Valerija Merker

Media partner Medienpartner
aspekte

Jury meeting
Jurysitzung
DAM Deutsches Architekturmuseum, Frankfurt am
Main

Members of the jury Mitglieder der Jury **2020**
Anett-Maud Joppien (Jury chairwoman
Juryvorsitzende), **Architect** Architektin/**Founding**
partner Gründungspartnerin **Dietz Joppien**
Planungsgesellschaft, Frankfurt am Main
Klaus Fäth, Structural Engineer Tragwerksplaner/
Founding partner Gründungspartner **office for**
structural design, Frankfurt am Main
Dr. Ina Hartwig, Deputy Mayor in Charge of Culture
Kulturdezernentin, **Frankfurt am Main**
Andreas Moser, Architect Architekt/**Founding partner**
Gründungspartner **Cyrus Moser Architekten, Frankfurt**
am Main
Benjamín Romano, Architect Architekt/**Founding**
partner Gründungspartner **LBR&A Arquitectos, Mexico**
City
Peter Cachola Schmal, Director Direktor **DAM**
Deutsches Architekturmuseum, Frankfurt am Main
Victor Stoltenburg, Managing Director
Geschäftsführer, **Deka Immobilien GmbH, Frankfurt am**
Main

Substitute member of the jury Stellvertretendes
Jurymitglied
Horst R. Muth, Head of Project & Development
Management Leiter Projektmanagement Immobilien,
Deka Immobilien GmbH, Frankfurt am Main

Consultant without a vote Berater ohne Stimmrecht
Rudi Scheuermann, Architect Architekt/**Director and**
Global Leader Building Envelope Design, Arup, Berlin

Imprint Catalog
Impressum Katalog

This catalog has been published in conjunction with
the exhibition "Best Highrises 2020/21", organized by
Deutsches Architekturmuseum, Department of Culture
and Science, Frankfurt am Main, Germany, taking
place from 31 October 2020 till 21 February 2021 at
Deutsches Architekturmuseum, Frankfurt am Main.
Dieser Katalog erscheint anlässlich der Ausstellung „Best
Highrises 2020/21" des Deutschen Architekturmuseums,
Dezernat Kultur und Wissenschaft, Stadt Frankfurt am
Main, vom 31. Oktober 2020 bis zum 21. Februar 2021
im Deutschen Architekturmuseum, Frankfurt am Main.

© 2020 by jovis Verlag GmbH

Cover Umschlagmotiv
Anders Bobert

Editors Herausgeber
Peter Körner, Stefanie Lampe, Jonas Malzahn,
Peter Cachola Schmal

Editing Redaktion
Peter Körner, Stefanie Lampe, Jonas Malzahn

Texts (unless otherwise stated) Texte (wenn nicht
anders angegeben)
Peter Körner, Stefanie Lampe, Jonas Malzahn

Copyediting (German) Lektorat (Deutsch)
Maike Kleihauer, Berlin

Copyediting (English) Lektorat (Englisch)
murphy translation office, Hamburg

Translation Übersetzung
murphy translation office, Hamburg (into English
ins Englische), **Miriam Seifert-Waibel, Hamburg**
(into German ins Deutsche)

Graphic design Gestaltung
Studio Joachim Mildner, Cologne Köln/**Zurich** Zürich

Coordination publishing house Koordination im Verlag
jovis, **Theresa Hartherz, Berlin**

Production Herstellung
jovis, **Susanne Rösler, Berlin**

Lithography Lithografie
Lars Scharrenbroich, Cologne Köln

Printing and binding Druck und Bindung
DZS Grafik, d. o. o., Ljubljana

Paper Papier
Galerie Art Volume, 150 g/qm

MIX
Paper from
responsible sources
FSC® C106600

Bibliographic information published by the Deutsche Nationalbibliothek
The Deutsche Nationalbibliothek lists this publication in the Deutsche Nationalbibliografie; detailed bibliographic data are available on the Internet at http://dnb.d-nb.de
Bibliografische Information der Deutschen Nationalbibliothek
Die Deutsche Nationalbibliothek verzeichnet diese Publikation in der Deutschen Nationalbibliografie; detaillierte bibliografische Daten sind im Internet über http://dnb.d-nb.de abrufbar.

jovis Verlag GmbH
Lützowstraße 33
10785 Berlin

www.jovis.de

jovis books are available worldwide in select bookstores. Please contact your nearest bookseller or visit www.jovis.de for information concerning distribution in your country.
jovis-Bücher sind weltweit im ausgewählten Buchhandel erhältlich. Informationen zu unserem internationalen Vertrieb erhalten Sie von Ihrem Buchhändler oder unter www.jovis.de.

ISBN 978-3-86859-644-1
(Retail edition Buchhandelsausgabe)

ISBN 978-3-86859-653-3
(Museum edition Museumsausgabe)

Imprint Exhibition
Impressum Ausstellung

Director Direktor DAM
Peter Cachola Schmal

Curators Kuratoren
Peter Körner, Stefanie Lampe, Jonas Malzahn

Exhibition design Ausstellungsgestaltung
Deserve Gbr Raum und Medien Design, Wiesbaden/Berlin, Mario Lorenz

Exhibition production Ausstellungsproduktion
inditec GmbH, Bad Camberg

Head of exhibition setup Leitung Ausstellungsaufbau
Christian Walter

Exhibition setup Ausstellungsaufbau
Marina Barry
Ulrich Diekmann
Jannik Hofmann
Leo Laduch
Eike Laeuen
Anke Menck
Jörn Schön
Ömer Simsek
Houaida Soubai
Gerhard Winkler

Registrar
Wolfgang Welker

Models Modelle
BIG – Bjarke Ingels Group, Copenhagen Kopenhagen
Heatherwick Studio, London
OMA Office for Metropolitan Architecture, Rotterdam/Beijing Peking
Oscar Properties, Stockholm
Skidmore, Owings & Merrill LLP, Chicago
Zaha Hadid Architects, London

Model restoration Modellrestaurierung
Christian Walter

Public relations Öffentlichkeitsarbeit
Brita Köhler, Anna Wegmann

Architectural Education Architekturvermittlung
Rebekka Kremershof

Guided tours Führungen
Yorck Förster

Administrative staff Sekretariat und Verwaltung
Inka Plechaty, Jacqueline Brauer

Graphic design print media Gestaltung Printmedien
Gardeners, Frankfurt am Main

Graphic design Picture-word mark
Gestaltung Bild-Wort-Marke
The International Highrise Award
Internationaler Hochhaus Preis
Studio Joachim Mildner, Cologne Köln/Zurich Zürich

For its generous funding and organizational support, DAM would like to thank its partner
Das DAM dankt dem Partner für die großzügige finanzielle und organisatorische Unterstützung
DekaBank
Sponsor of the International Highrise Award and the exhibition
Sponsor des Internationalen Hochhaus Preises und der Ausstellung

With special thanks to
Mit besonderem Dank an
Camille Abeille, Colette Aro, Fadi Asmar, Allison Ball, Tess Beckingham, Jerzy Behnke, Malin Berden, Kai-Uwe Bergmann, Karen Blyth, Andrea Chin, Deborah Churchill, Meredith Coco, Siân Confrey, Linus Creuzer, Annie Croll, Natalie Dargham, David Davila, Yolanta Duran Montoro, Javier Exposito, Kjell Fallqvist, Annika Frey, Petra Funk, Jesslyn Guntur, Katy Harris, Andrew James, Sarah John, Kalina Kalarus
Serena Khor, Chrlotte Kruk, Andrea Lamberti, Raymond Lee, Jelena Loncar, Jaron Lubin, Elin Martin, Gayle Mault, Véronique Moine, Christine Noblejas, Daria Pahhota, Tae-Ry Park, Michele Pasca di Magliano, Robyn Payne, Adrienne Peñaloza, Stephan Pflaum, Dale Potts, Alexandru Retegan, Dolores Robles Martínez Gómez, Adam Ross, Sandra Staab, Linda Stewart, Claudia Tiesler, Stephanie Tsang, Zhaoming Wang, Märit Wilkström, Sylvia Wong, Anna Yeboah, Dukho Yehon, Nora Zerelli, Christina Zhuang, Kui Zhuang